ALL IN A DAY'S WORK

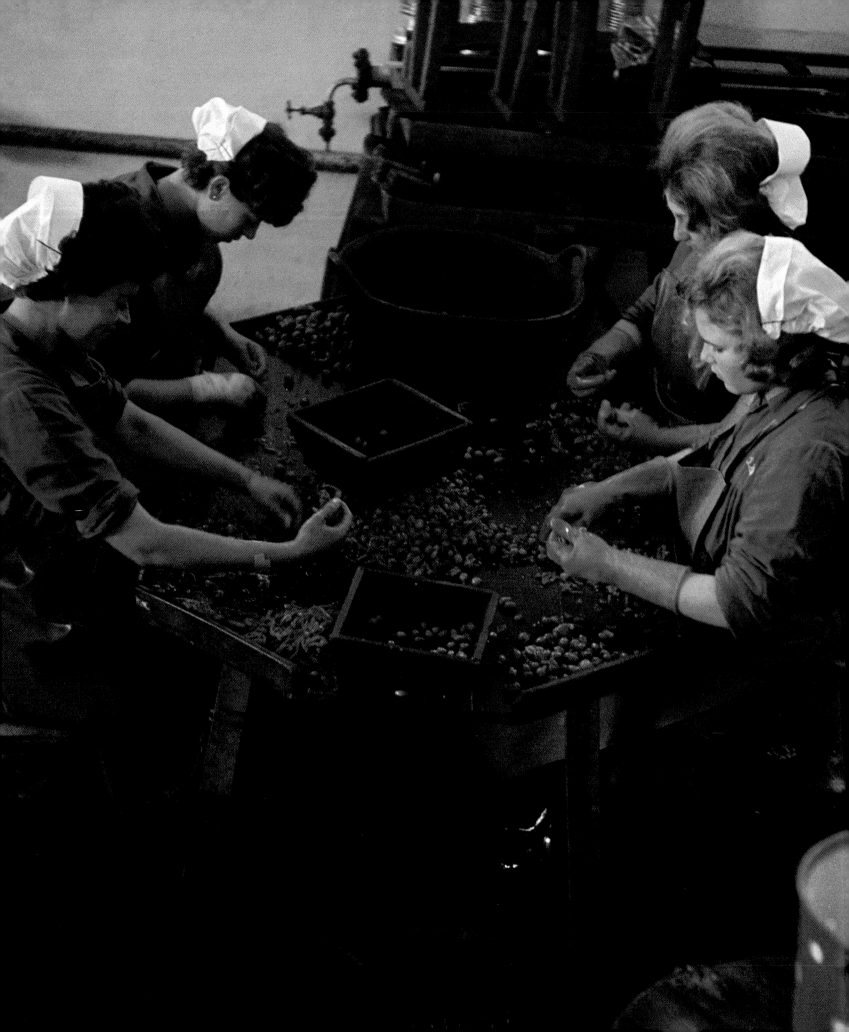

EVE ARNOLD

ALL IN A DAY'S WORK

HAMISH HAMILTON LTD
LONDON

JACKET COVER

INNER MONGOLIA   Equestrian acrobats rehearsing

FRONTISPIECE

SPAIN   Stuffing pimientos into olives

HAMISH HAMILTON LTD

Published by the Penguin Group
27 Wrights Lane, London W8 5TZ, England
Viking Penguin Inc., 40 West 23rd Street, New York, New York 10010, U.S.A.
Penguin Books Australia Ltd, Ringwood, Victoria, Australia
Penguin Books Canada Ltd, 2801 John Street, Markham, Ontario, Canada L3R 1B4
Penguin Books (N.Z.) Ltd, 182-190 Wairau Road, Auckland 10, New Zealand

Penguin Books Ltd, Registered Offices: Harmondsworth, Middlesex, England

First published in Great Britain 1990 by
Hamish Hamilton Ltd
First published in the United States 1989 by Bantam Books,
a division of Bantam Doubleday Dell Publishing Group, Inc.
Copyright © 1989 by Eve Arnold

10 9 8 7 6 5 4 3 2 1

CIP data for this book is available from the British Library

ISBN 0-241-12643-6

TO MY GRANDSON MICHAEL WITH LOVE

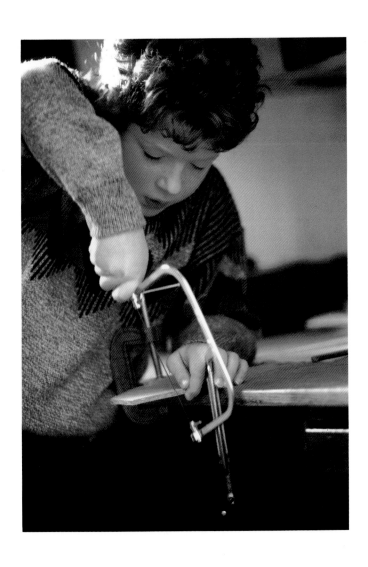

"...the only thing a man can do

for eight hours a day,

day after day, is work.

You can't eat for eight hours a day

nor drink for eight hours a day,

nor make love for eight hours."

—WILLIAM FAULKNER

For the past thirty-five years I have photographed
people at work—from Zululand to Afghanistan.
During my travels I sought out an endless succession of
jobs and professions, cerebral and physical, to film.
Work for me became an all-consuming subject.
It was natural to the camera—a deep reflection of
the culture and the industrial development of countries
through which I passed. It spoke of primitive skills,
of vanishing crafts and technologies beyond most
people's experience.

In this documentation I could see fragments of our past,
our present, our future. These pictures, born of a
private passion, became a personal cache to enjoy
when I returned from professional assignments. They were
personal work made for my pleasure, without any of the
restrictions that surround work for hire. They became
a kaleidoscope through which to view the way we relate
to our world, the way we work to live and live to work.

Eve Arnold, 1989

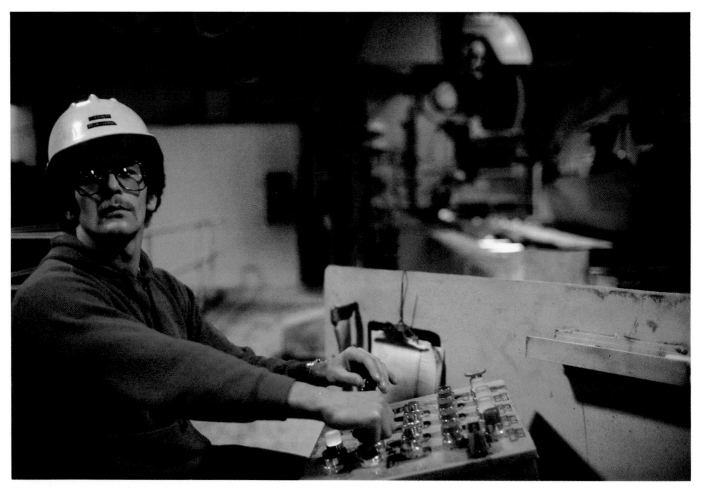

UNITED STATES
Operating a control panel in a lumber mill

SOUTH AFRICA
Gold miner after a grueling day underground

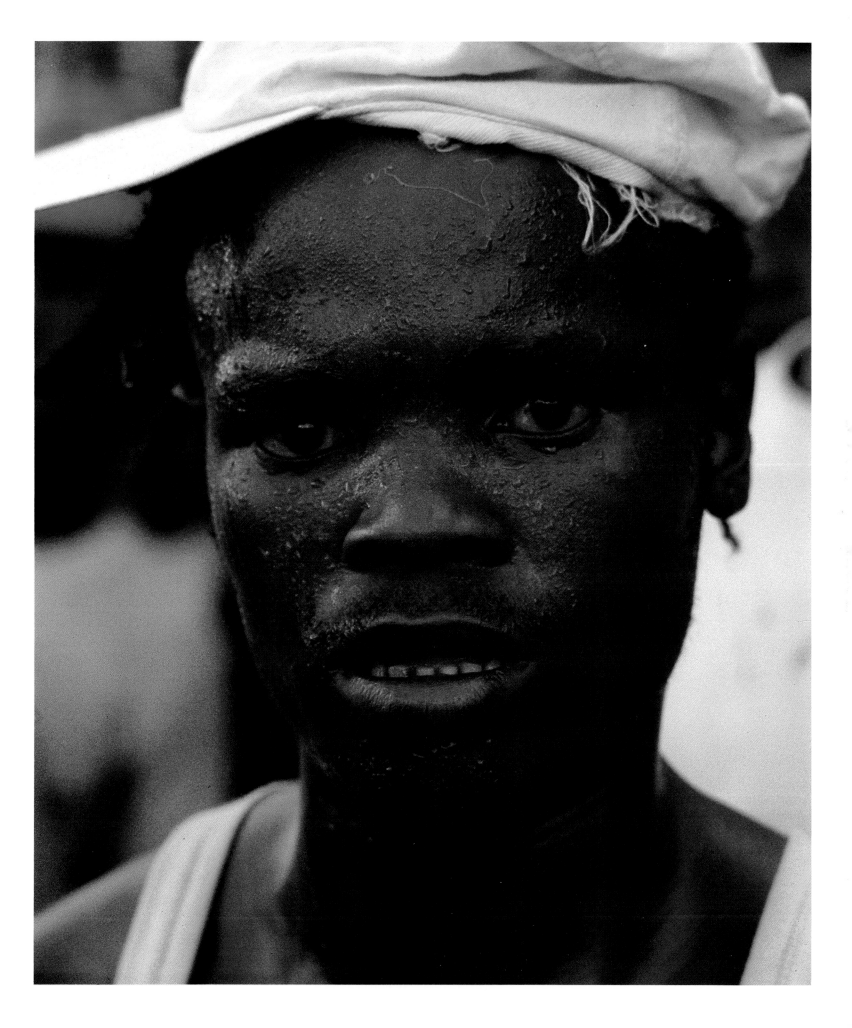

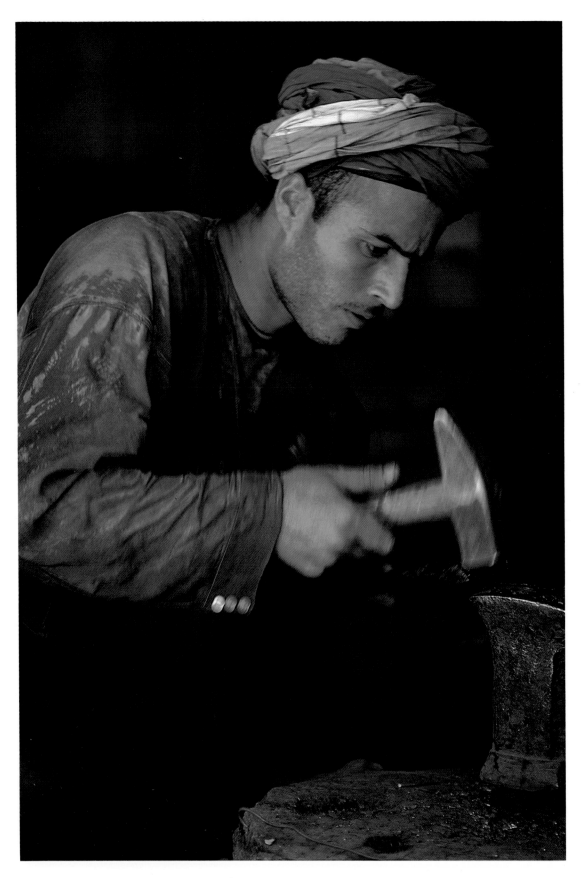

PAKISTAN
An ironworker wields a hammer   10

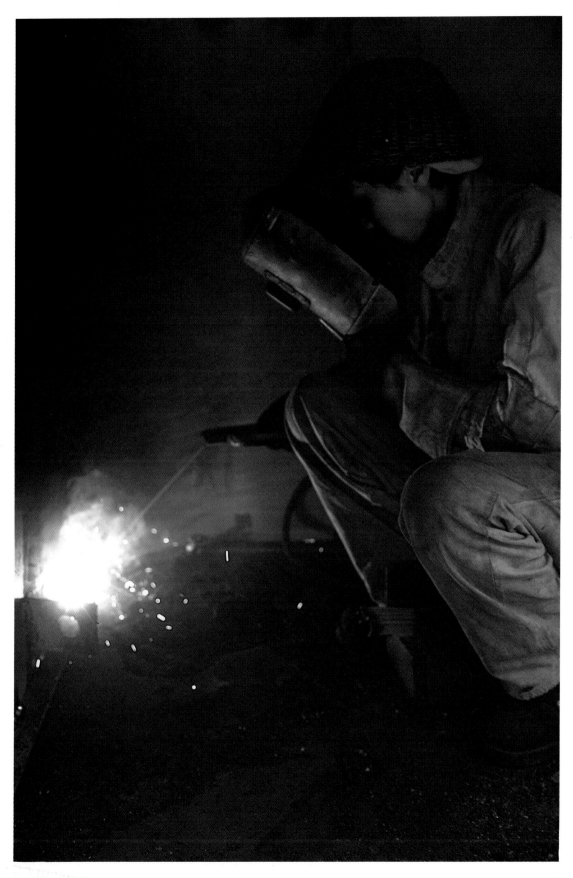

A welder in a shipyard

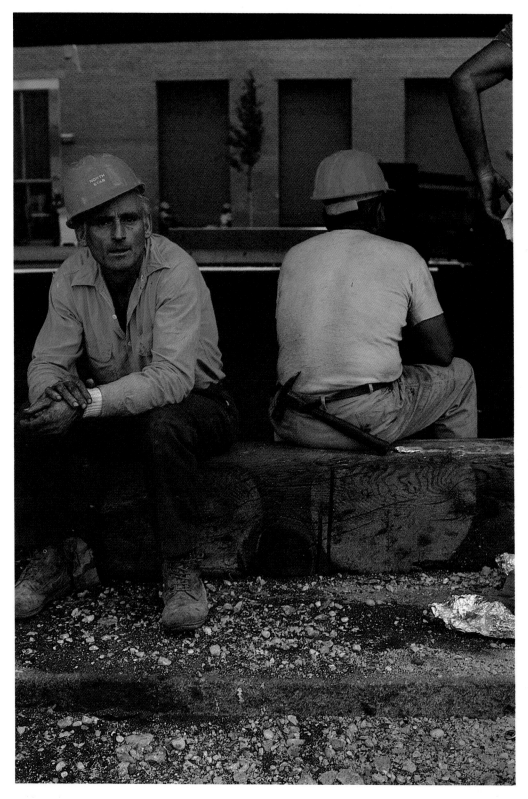

UNITED STATES
Lunch break on the construction site

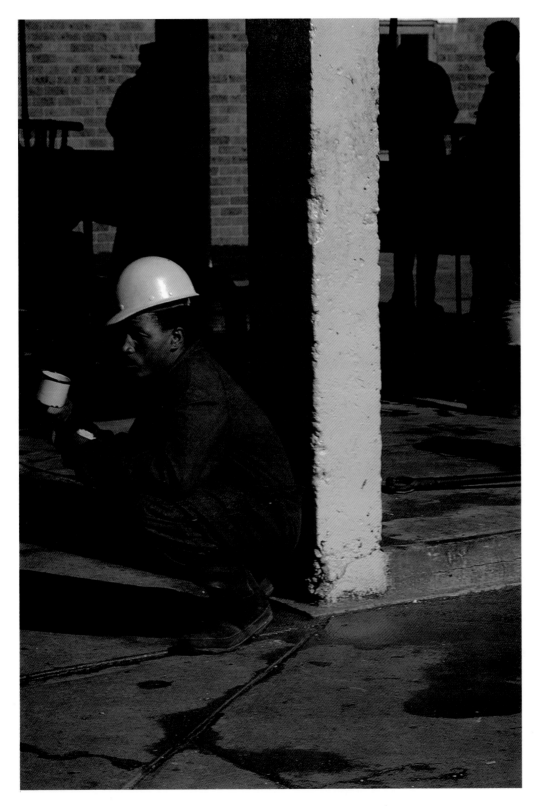

SOUTH AFRICA
Resting at the Val Reef Gold Mines

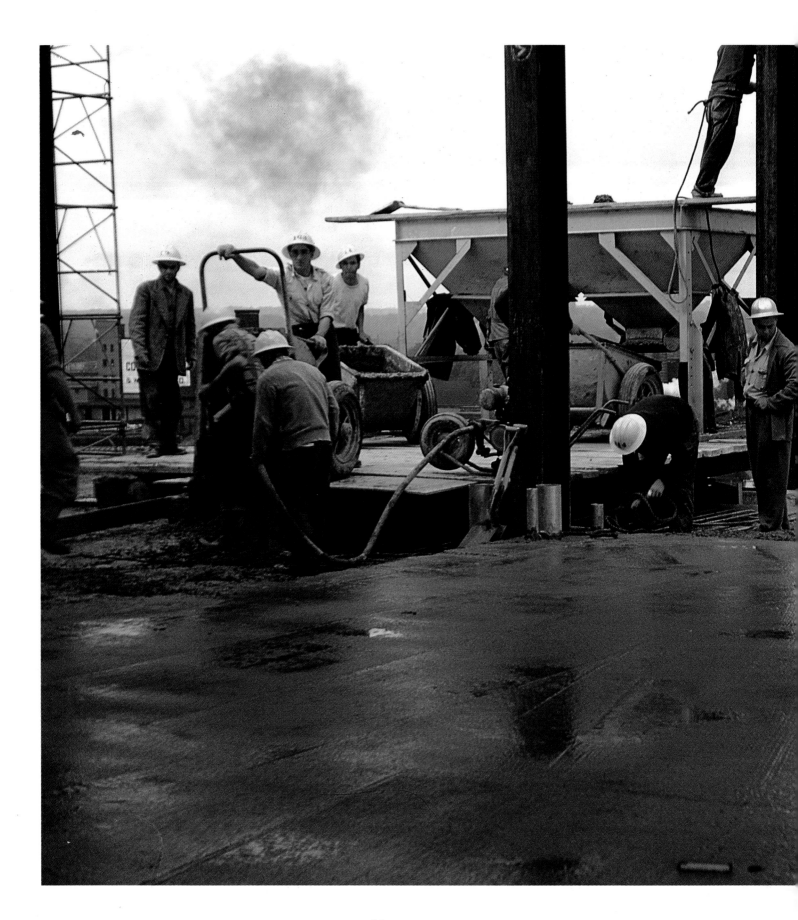

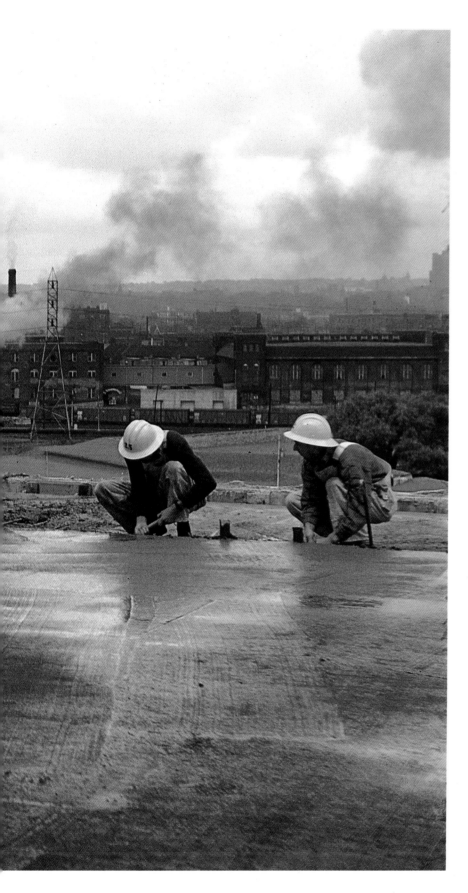

Building a hotel in Toronto

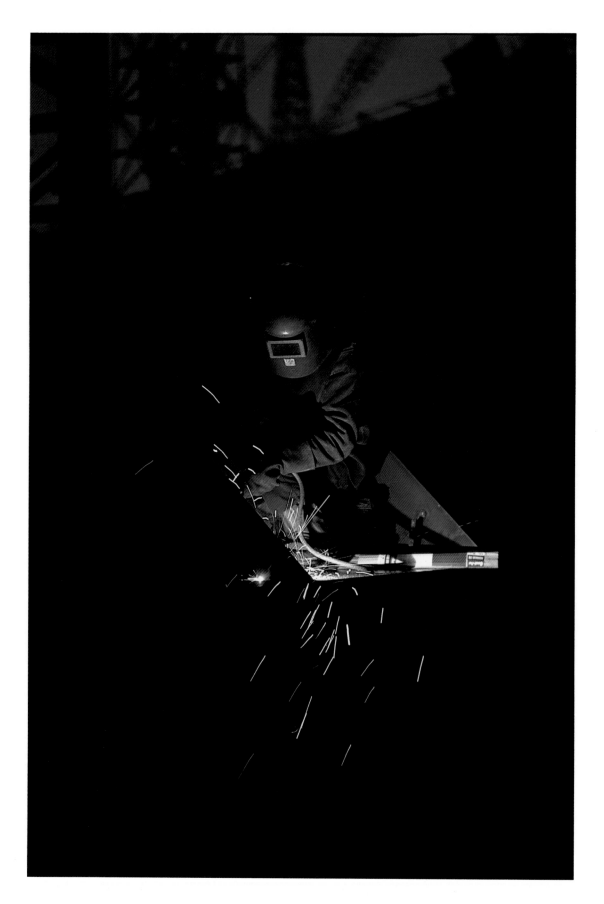

"Why do you work only four days a week?"

Reply: "Because I cannot live on what I make in three."

—BRITISH COAL MINER

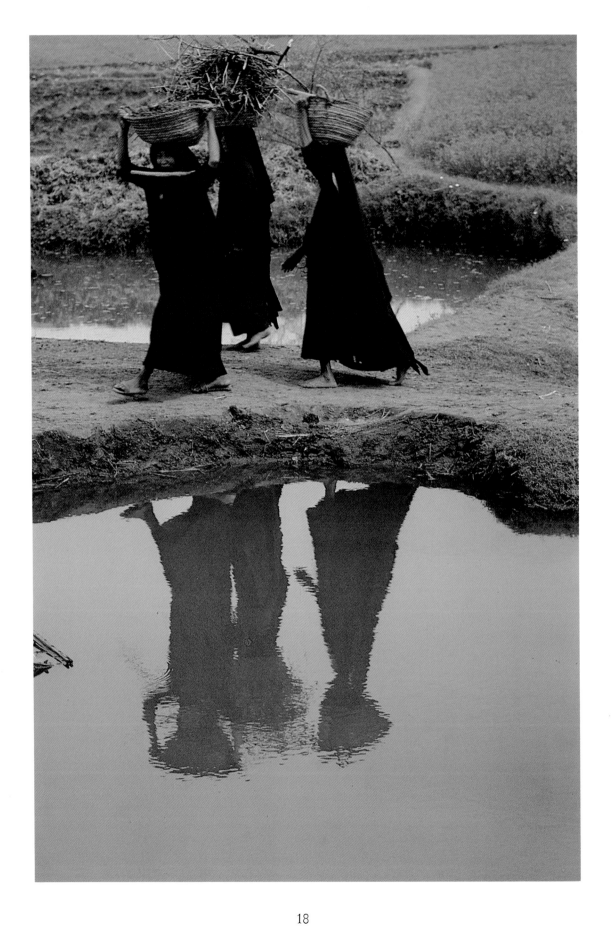

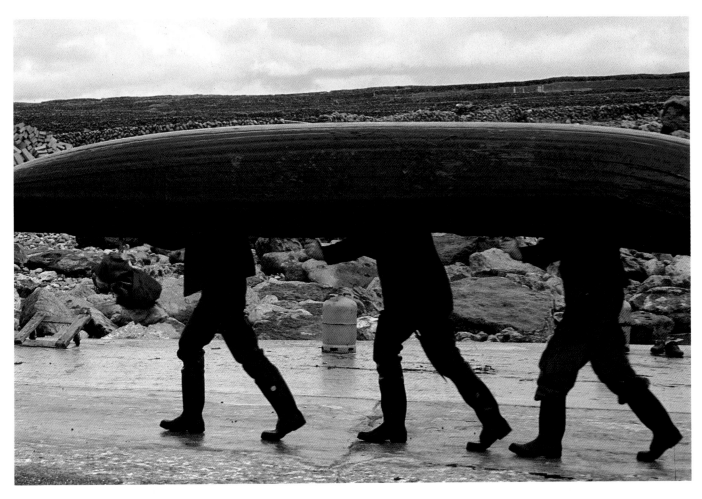

ARAN ISLANDS
Carrying a curragh down to the ship that brings
the community's weekly supplies

EGYPT
Along the Nile, women carry home firewood to
cook the evening meal

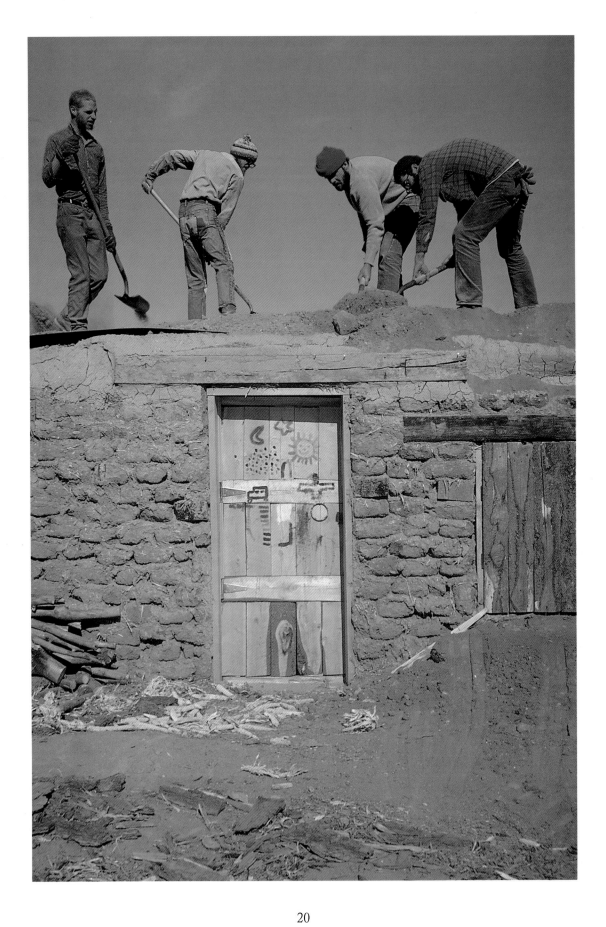

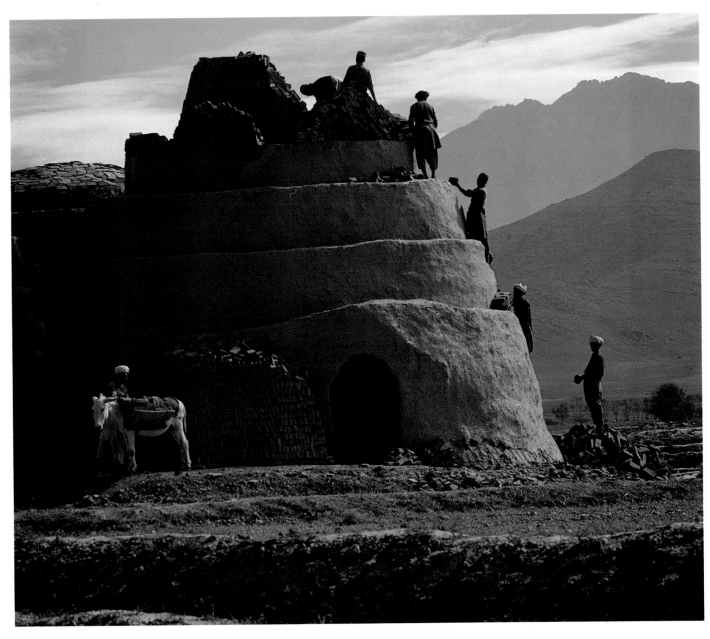

AFGHANISTAN
Making bricks in the Hindu Kush

UNITED STATES
Building a communal dwelling

"Honest labor bears a lovely face."

—Thomas Dekker

China
Tea picker on the Laotian border

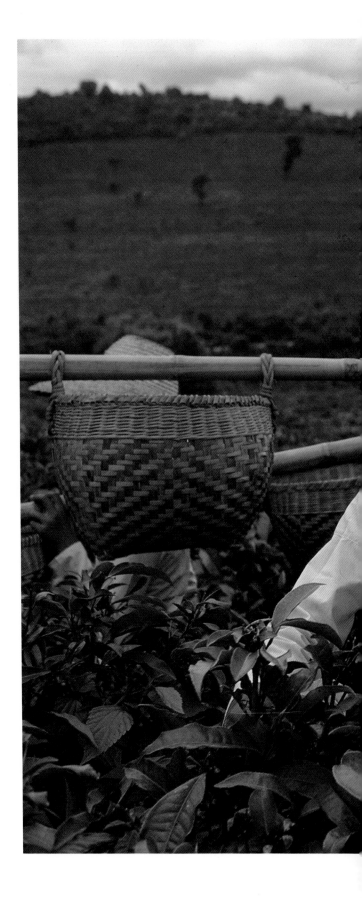

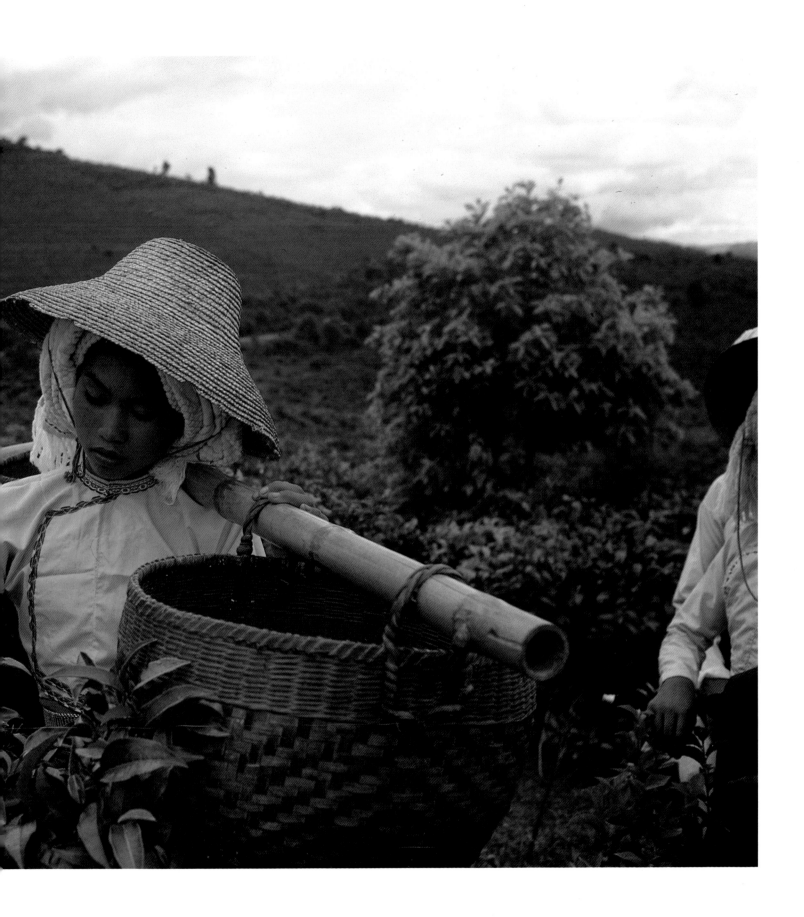

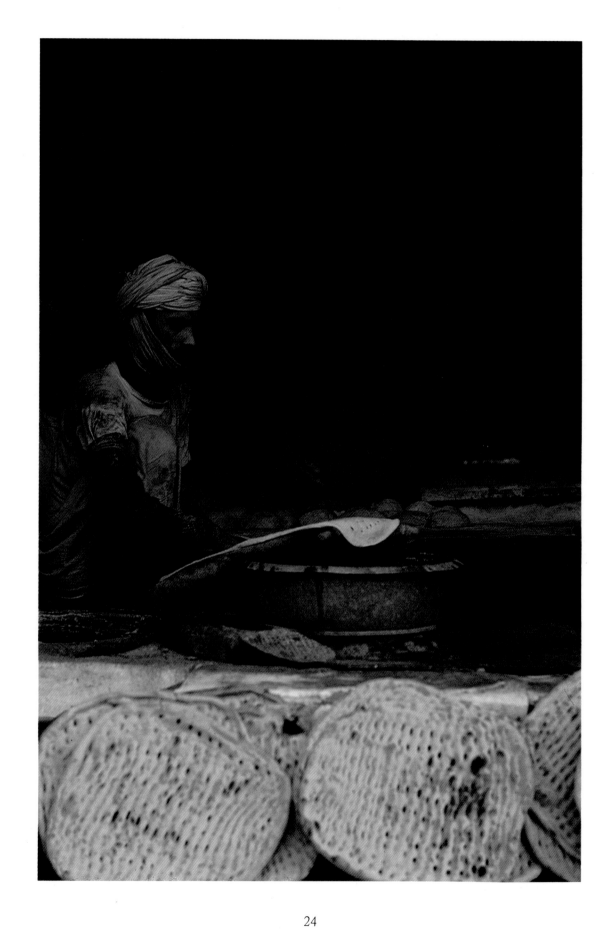

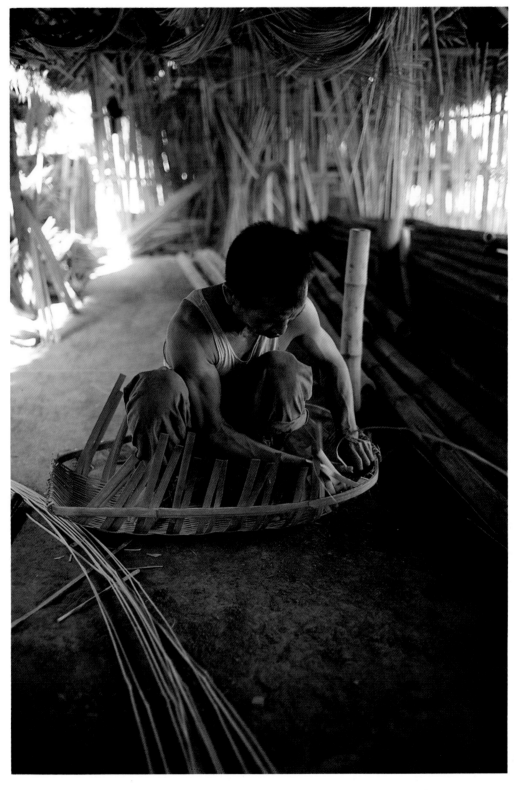

CHINA
Basket weaving

AFGHANISTAN
Baking the daily bread in a tandoori oven

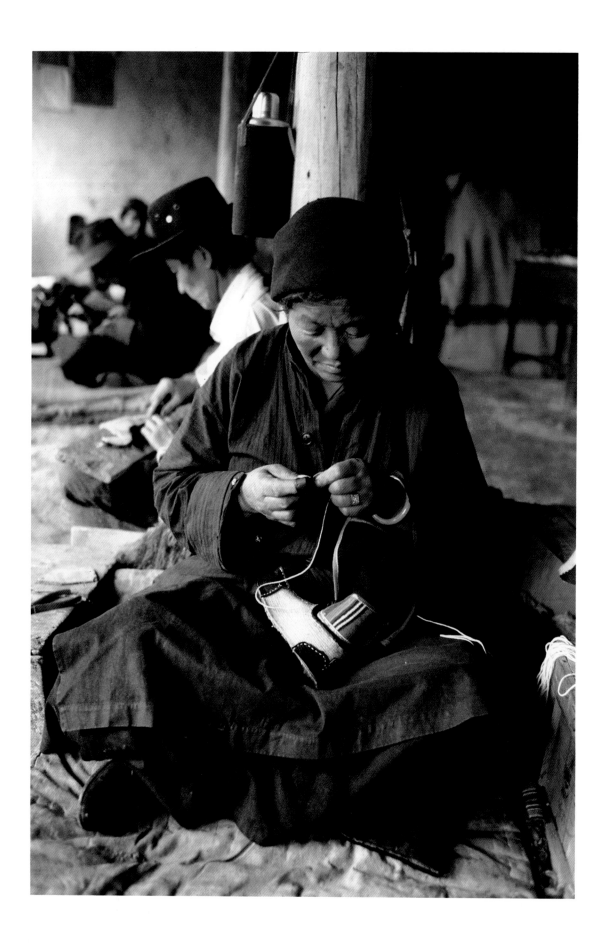

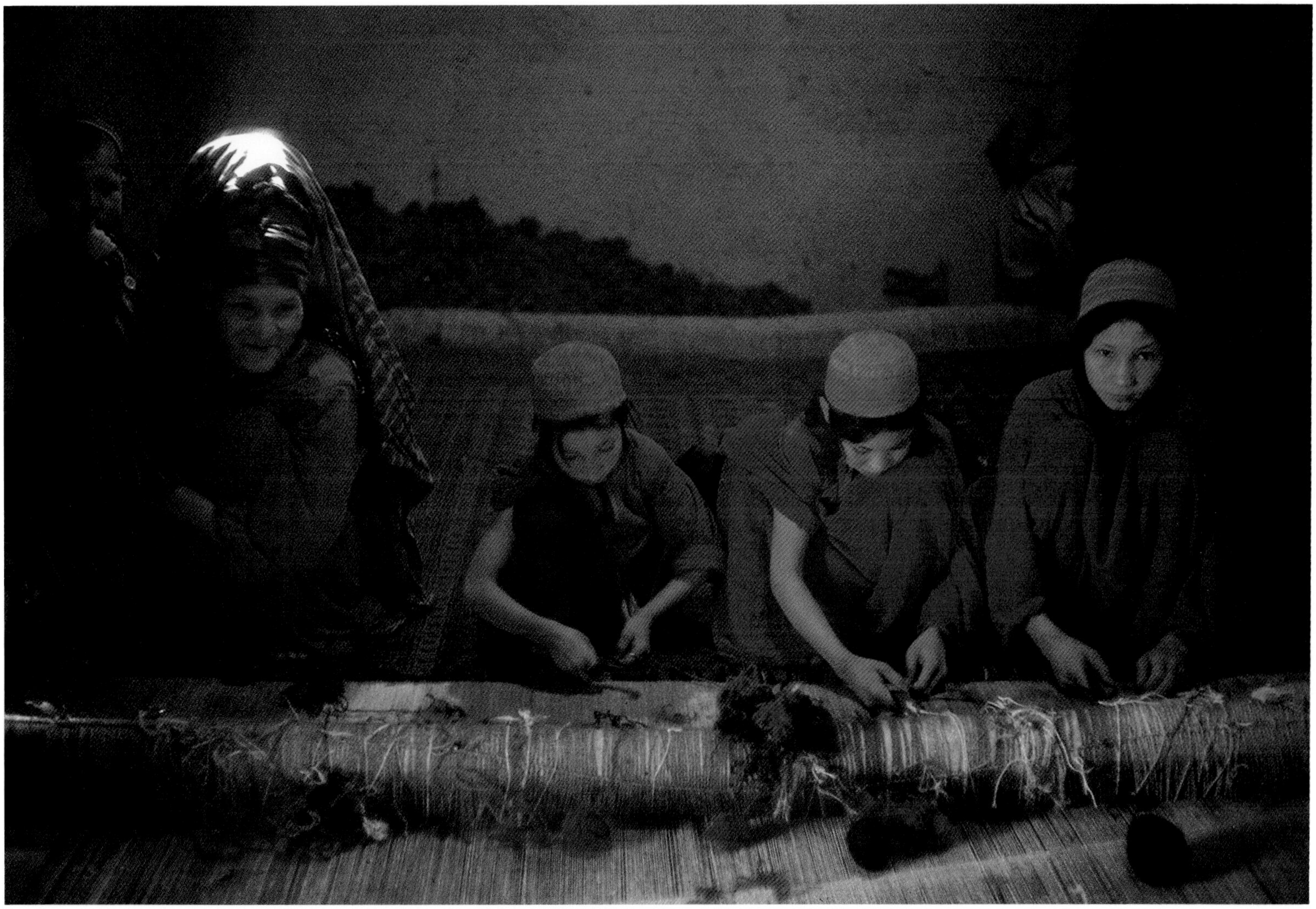

TURKESTAN
The women of the family weave a rug

TIBET
Making shoes

"I tell you, sir, the only safeguard of order and discipline in the modern

world is a standardized worker with interchangeable parts."

—Jean Giradoux

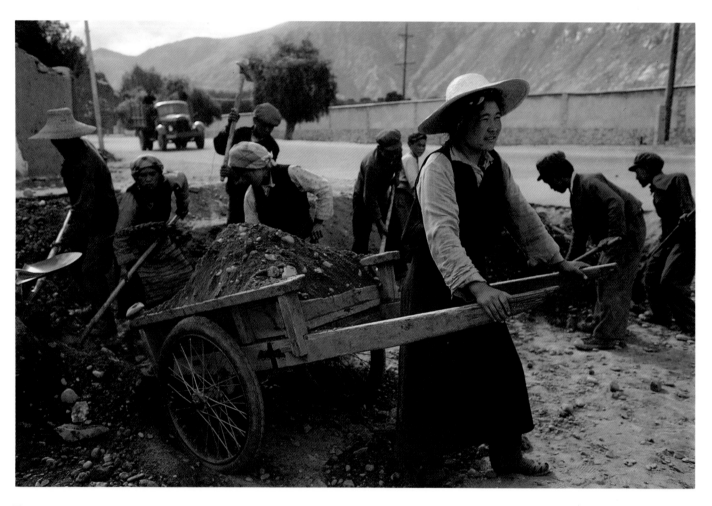

Tibet
A construction crew builds a road

Pakistan
Garage mechanics take dents out of fenders

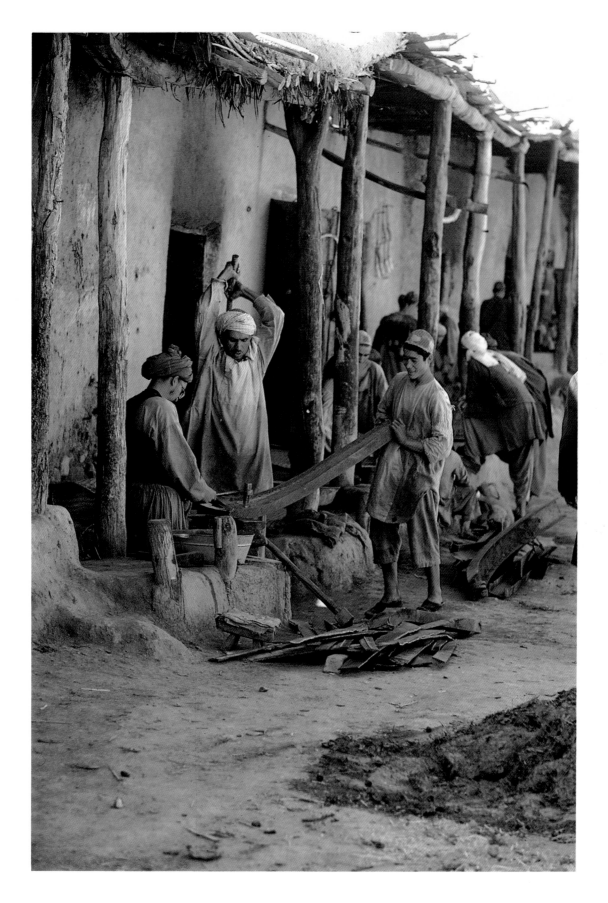

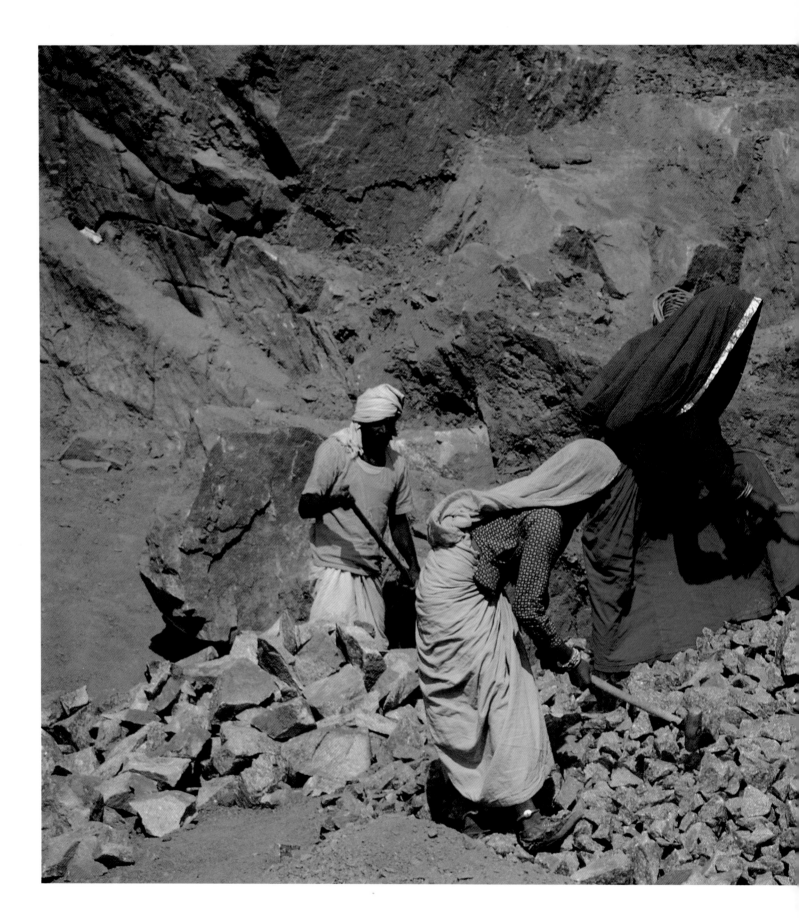

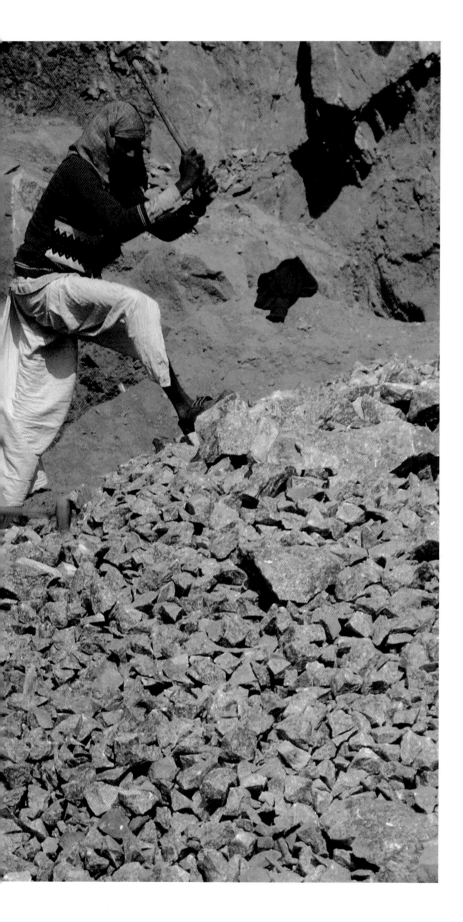

"Which of us—is to do the hard
and dirty work for the rest—
and for what pay?"

—John Ruskin

INDIA
Breaking rock at a quarry in New Delhi

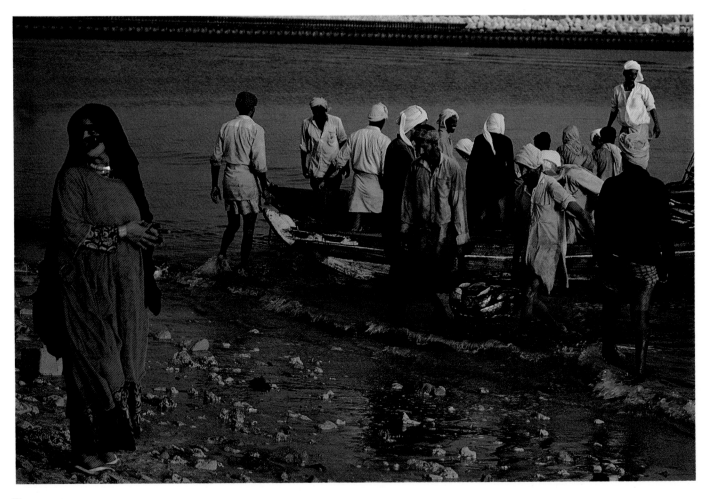

DUBAI
Fishermen bring in the catch for the woman who is their employer

TUNISIA
A sailor

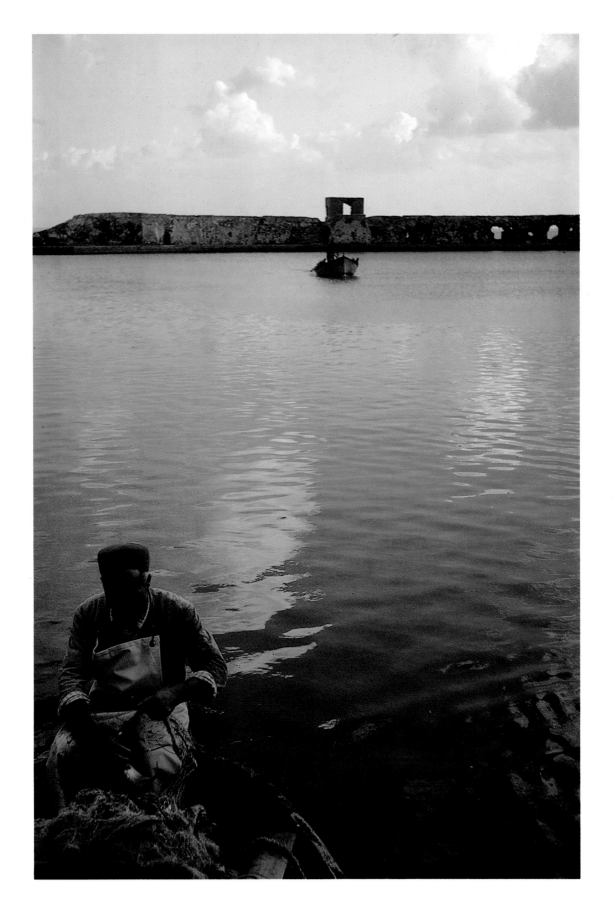

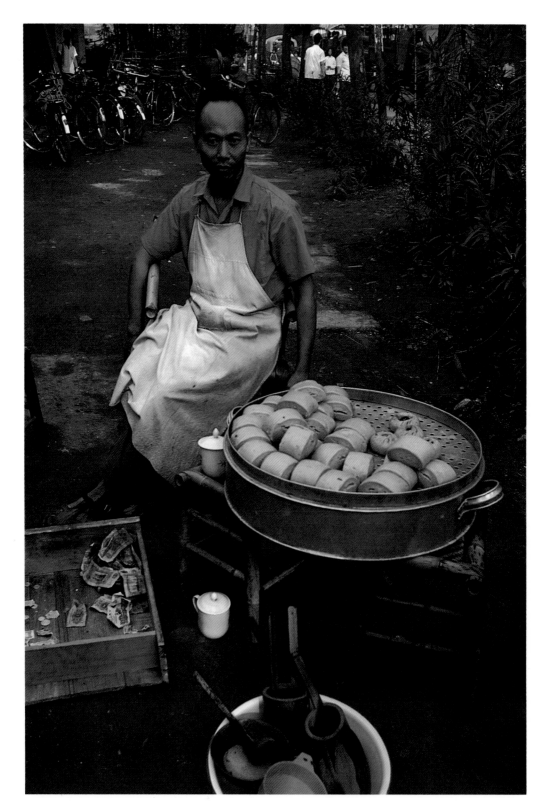

CHINA
Selling steamed bread

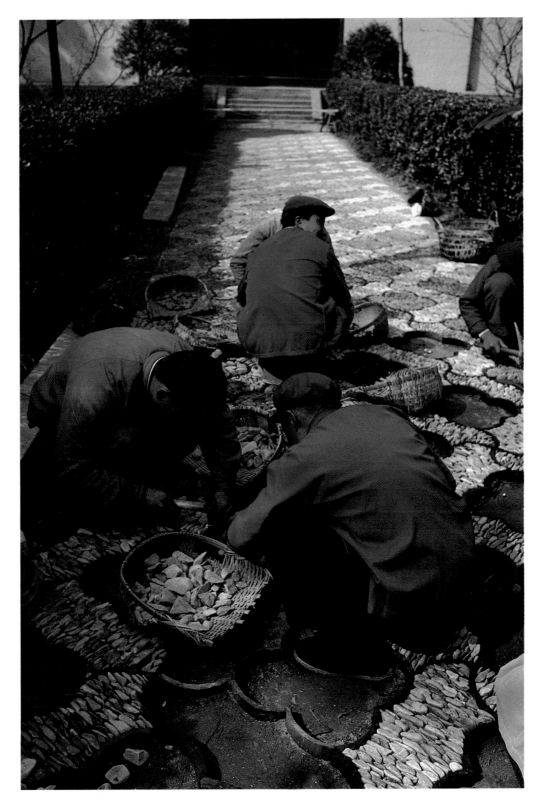

CHINA
Tile setters lay a new entrance to a temple

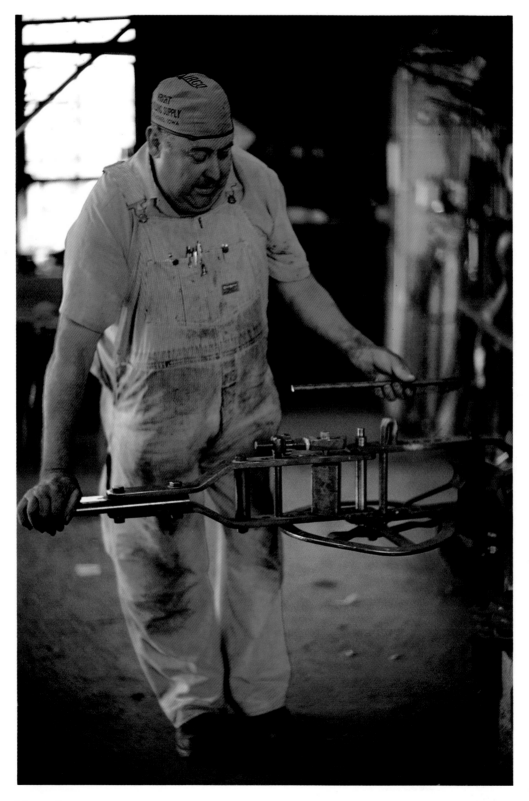

U.S.S.R.
Beekeeper

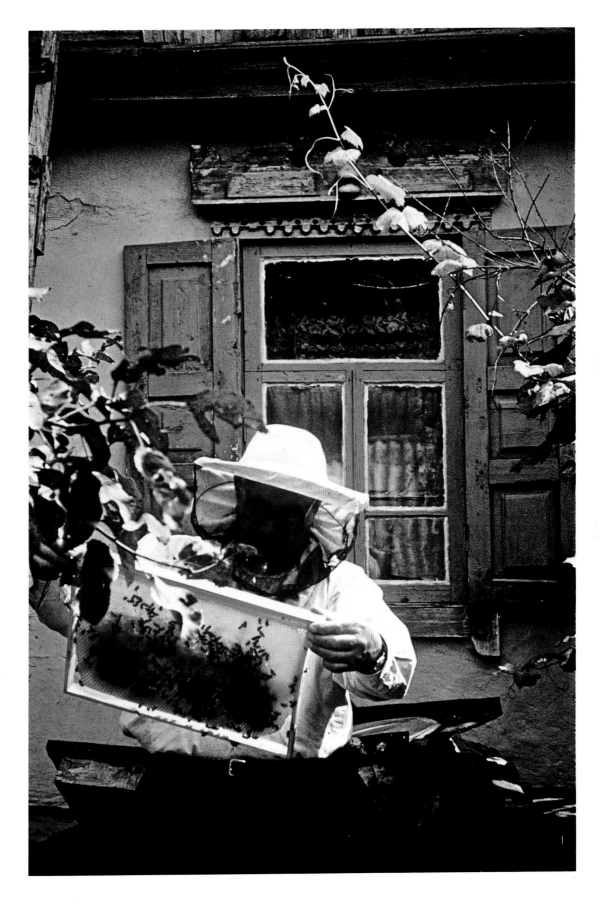

*"I felt then and I still feel that the purpose
of life must be more than going to work,
coming home and going to bed. I don't believe
in the work ethic. I don't believe in the rich man,
poor man lie about the 'dignity of labor.'
There's no more dignity in labor than there
is in not working. I never felt ashamed to
be out of work: I just felt broke."*

—Bob Geldof, *Is That It?*

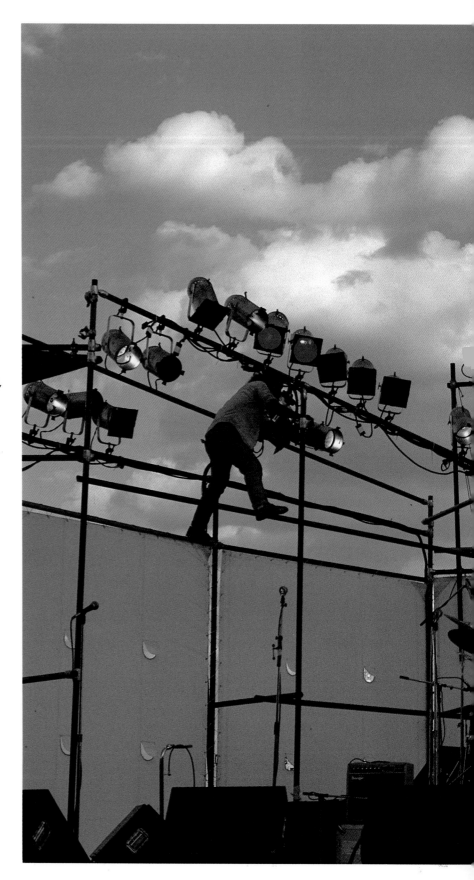

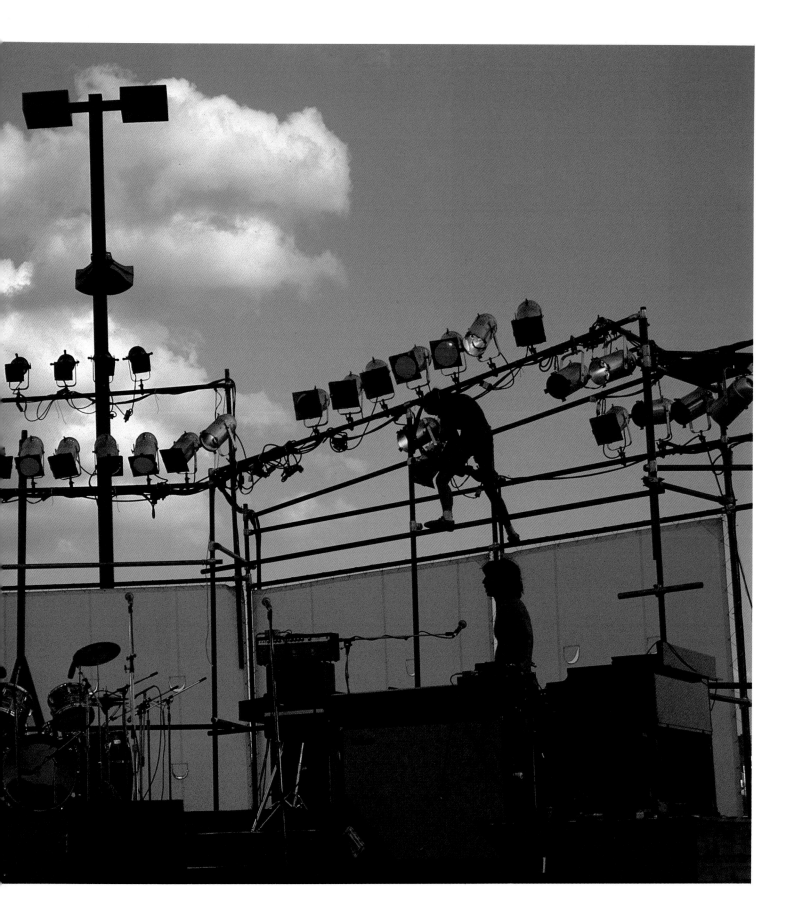

"Every man's work, whether it be literature or music or pictures or architecture or anything else, is always a portrait of himself, and the more he tries to conceal himself the more clearly will his character appear in spite of him."

—SAMUEL BUTLER,
The Way of All Flesh

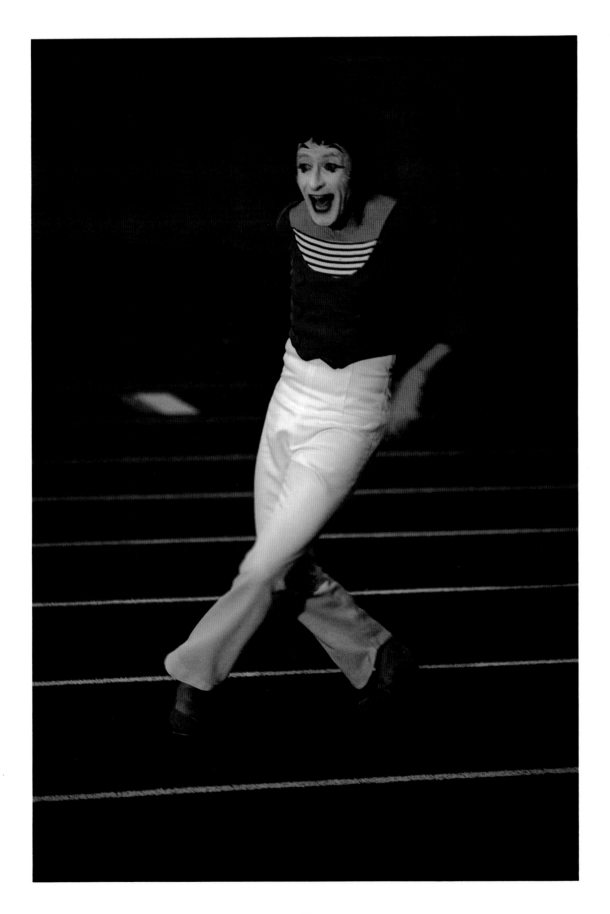

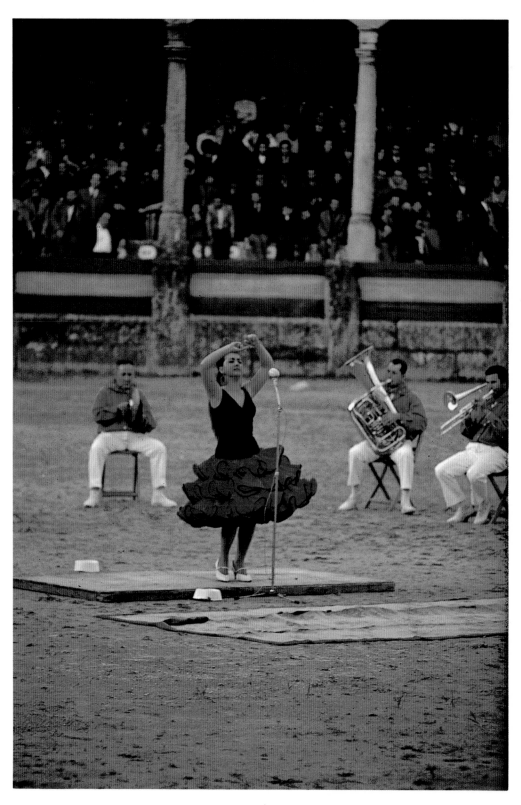

SPAIN
Flamenco dancer and acrobats in the world's oldest-
known bull ring at Ronda

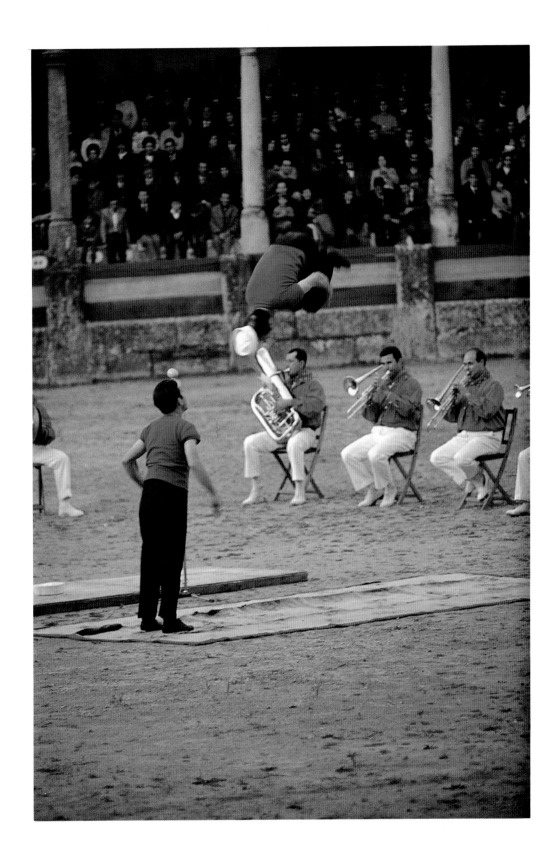

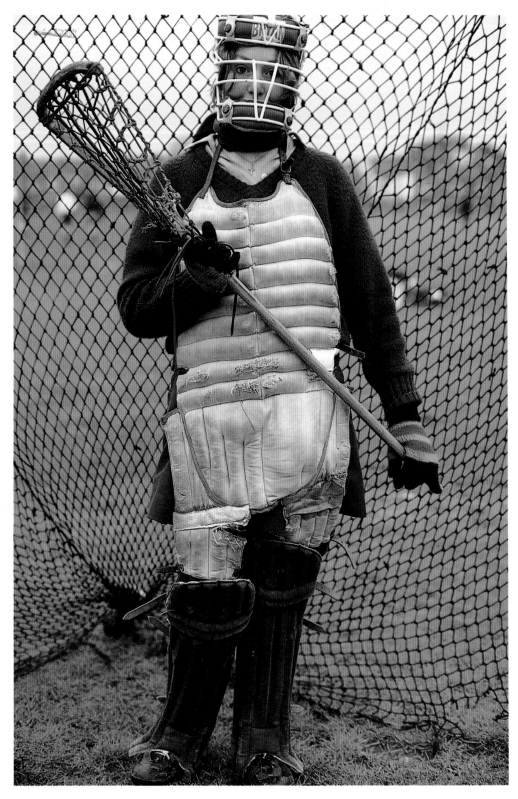

ENGLAND
Lacrosse at a girls' private school

UNITED STATES
Baseball game between the Chicago Cubs and the Atlanta Braves

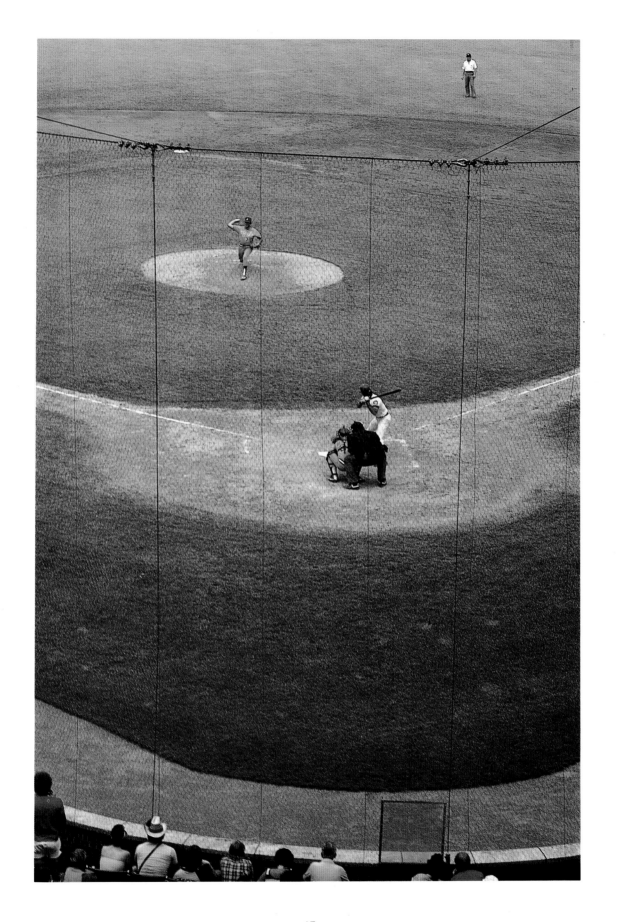

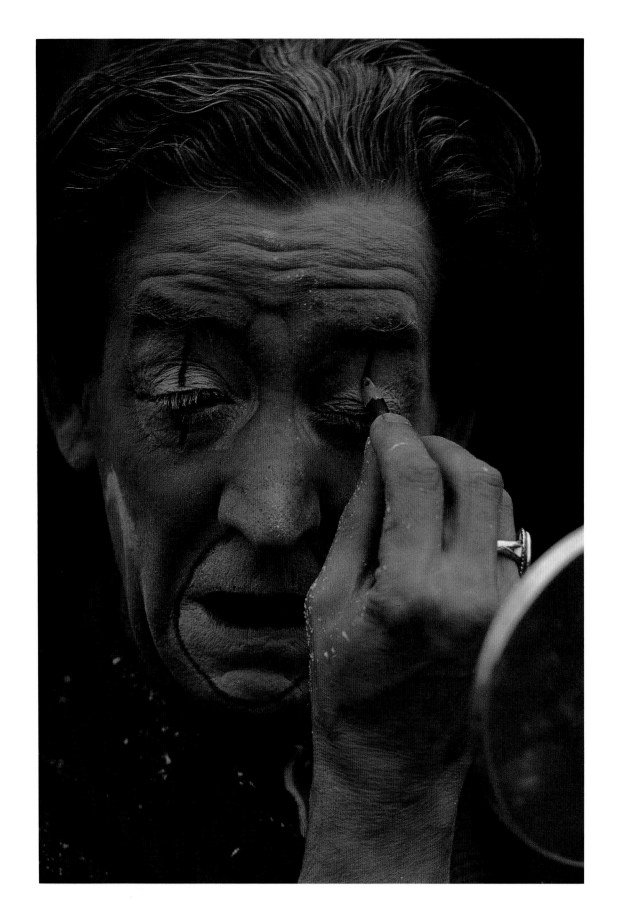

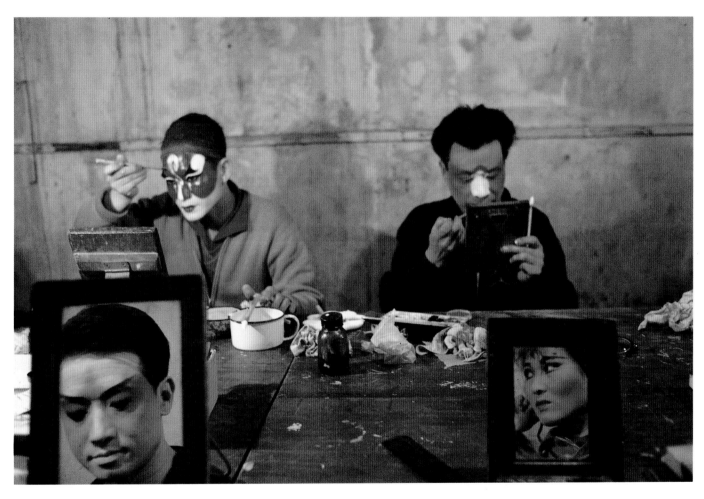

CHINA
Actors making up for an opera performance

SCOTLAND
A clown making up for the circus

ENGLAND
Charles Chaplin sets up a shot during the filming
of *A Countess from Hong Kong*

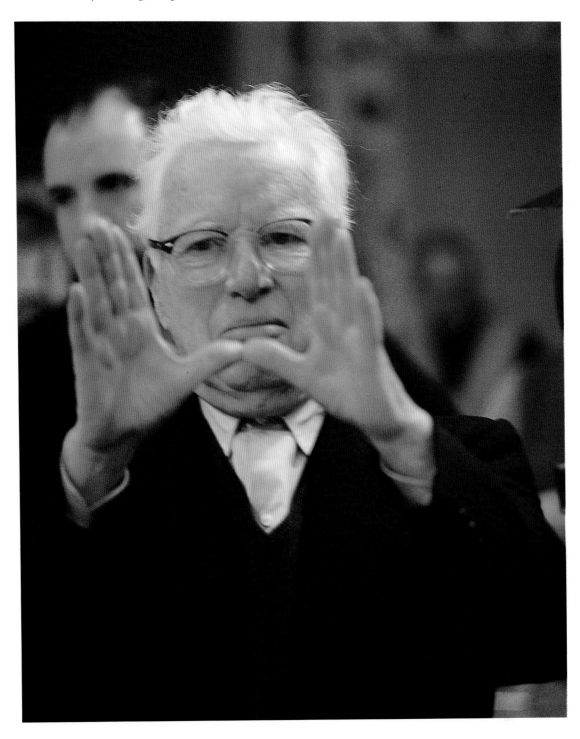

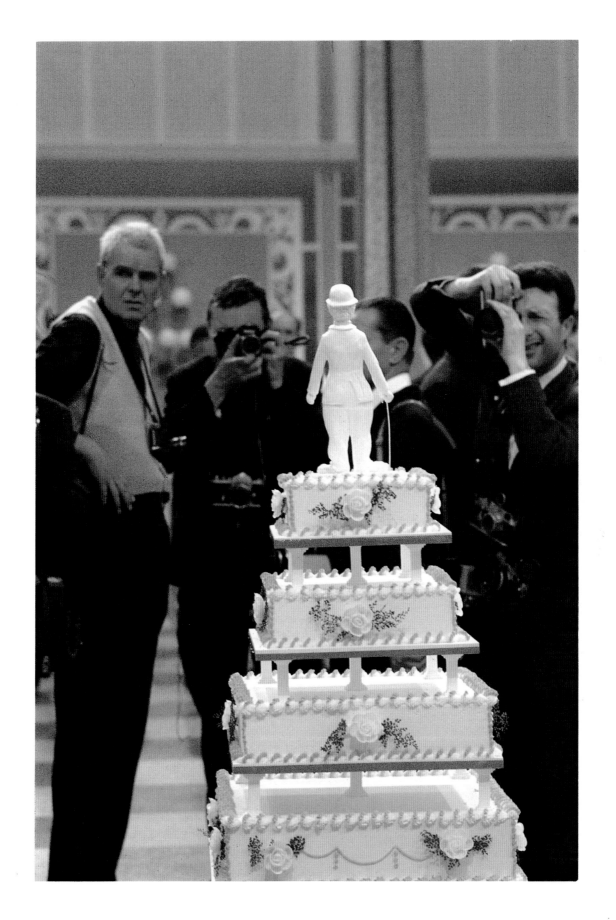

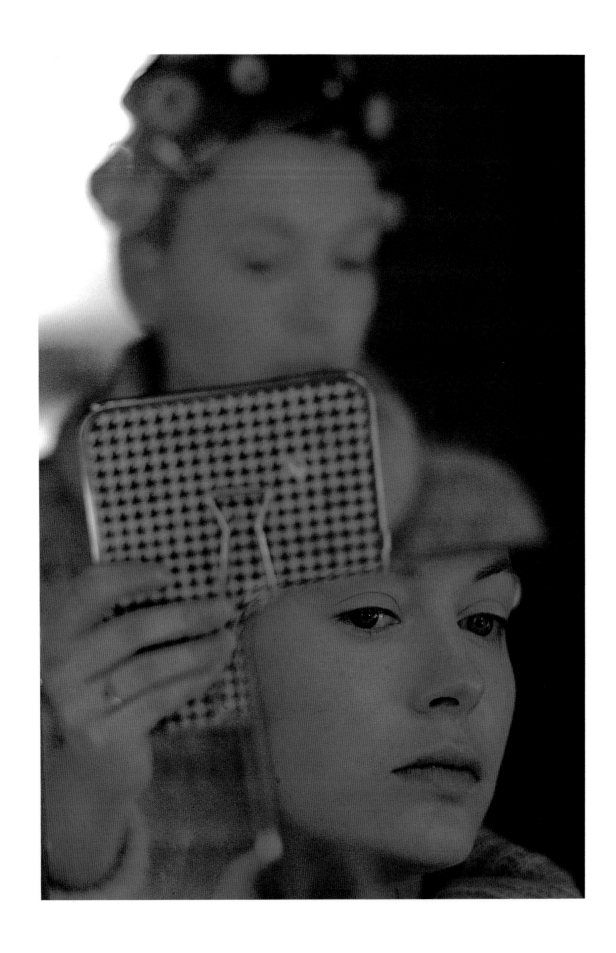

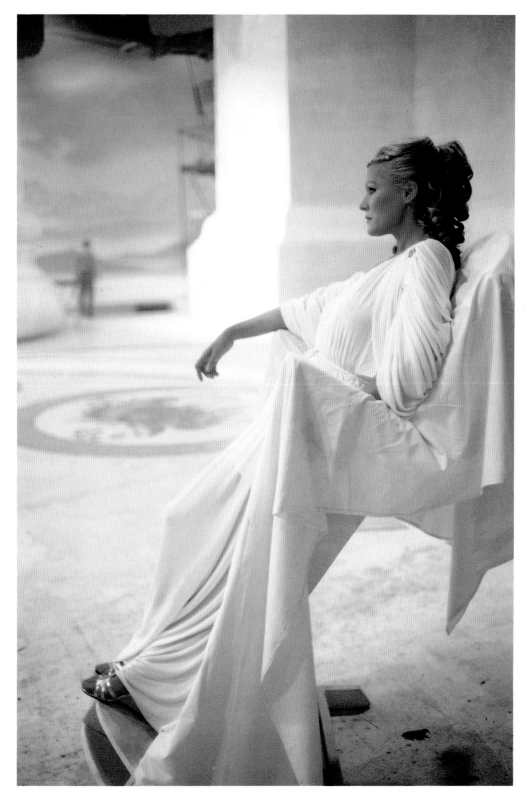

IRELAND
Actress Lesley Ann Down
makes up for the film
The Great Train Robbery

ENGLAND
On the set of *Clash of the Titans*, Ursula Andress
leans against a board to avoid creasing her robe

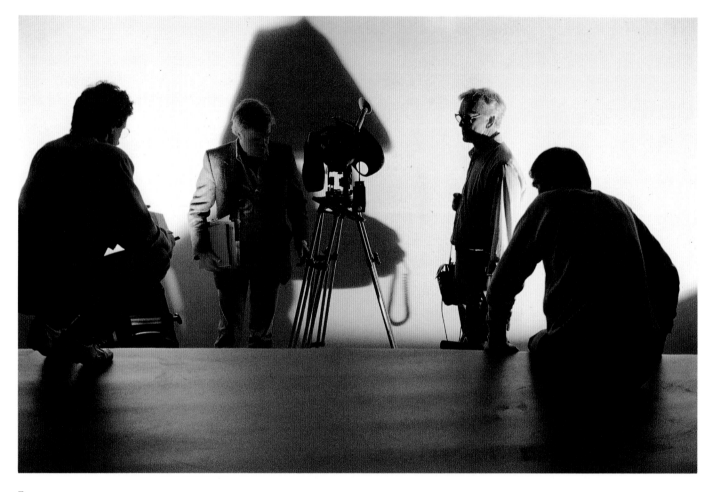

FINLAND
A BBC crew

PAKISTAN
A street photographer plying his trade

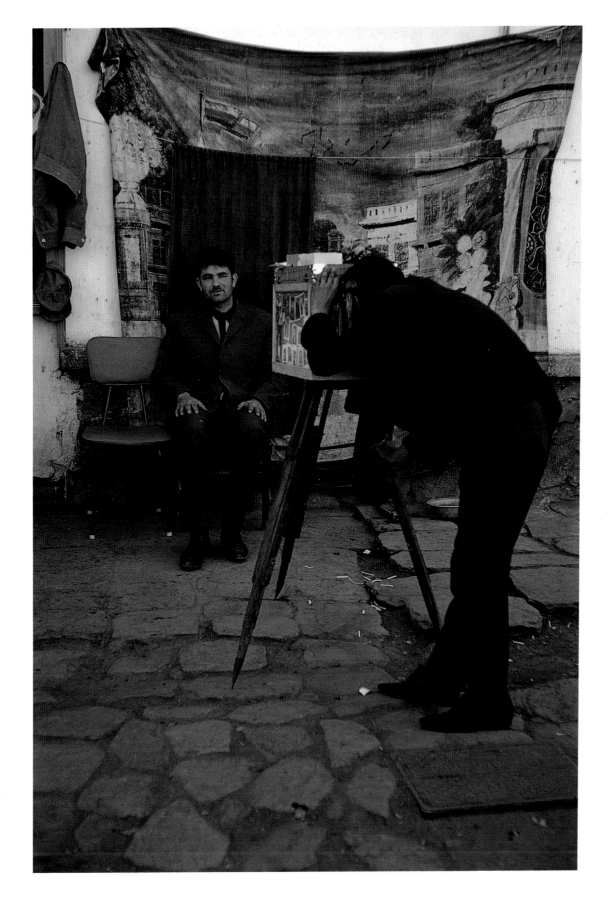

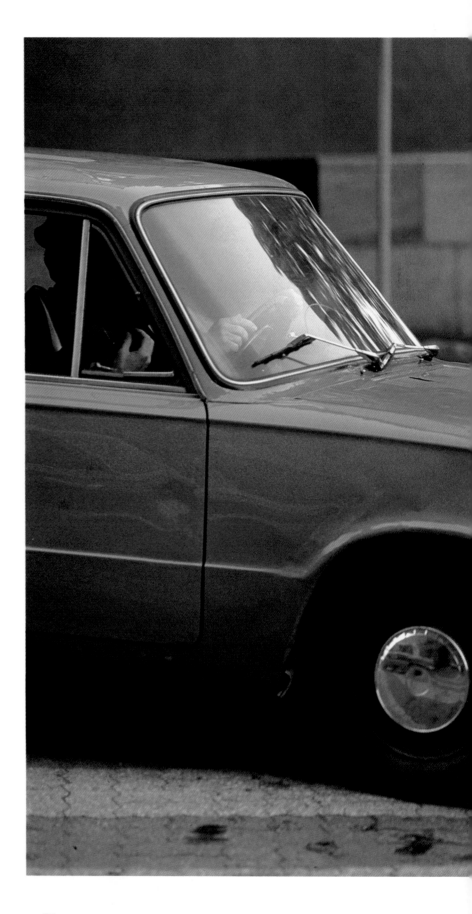

"No man is born into the world whose work
Is not born with him; there is always work,
And tools to work withal, for those who will."

—James Russell Lowell

Finland
A movie soundman between two cars, recording
sound for the film *White Nights*

54

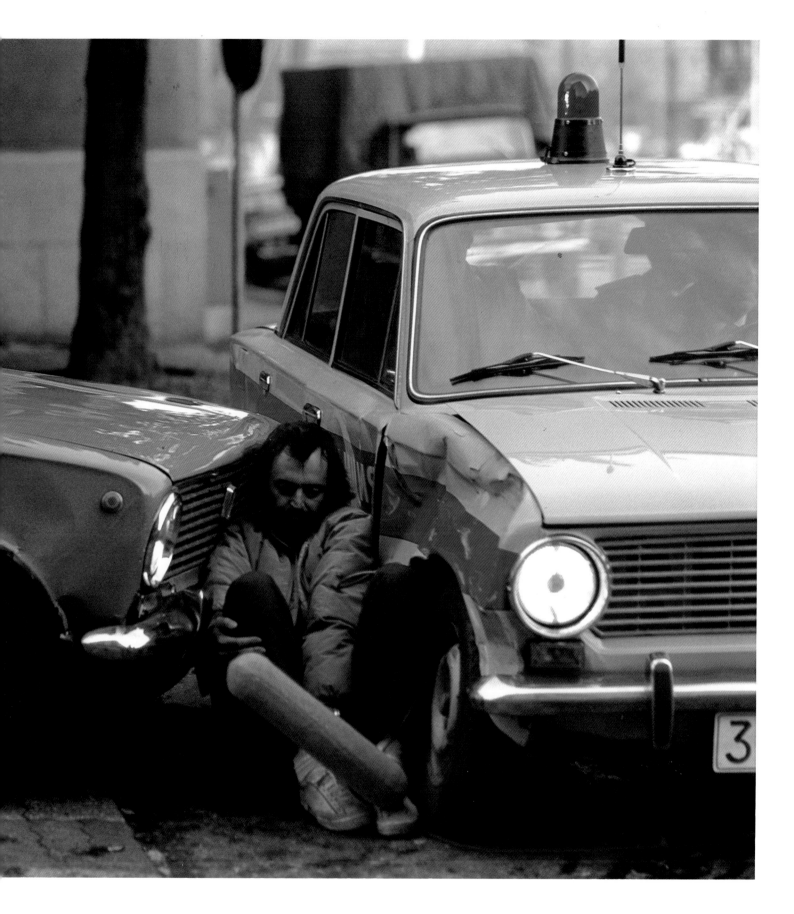

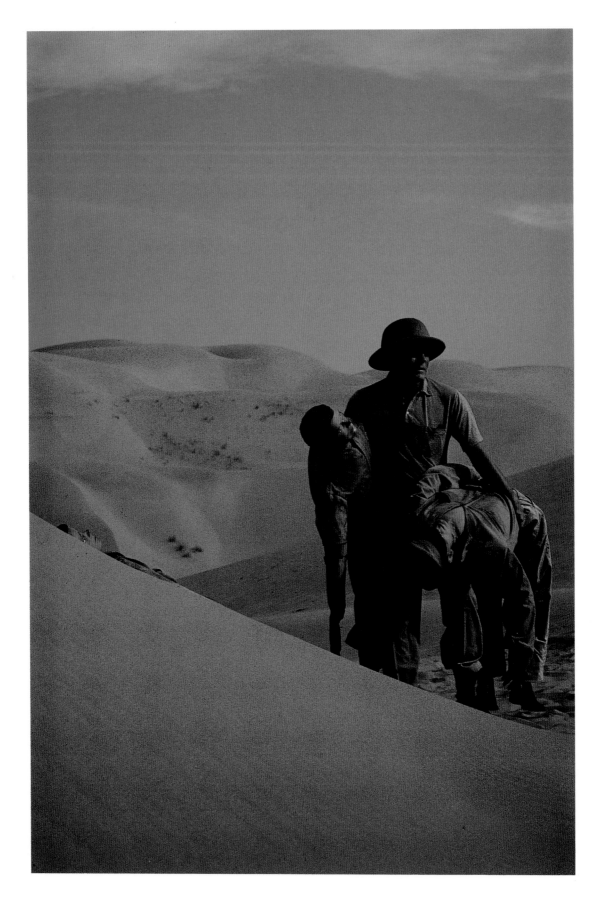

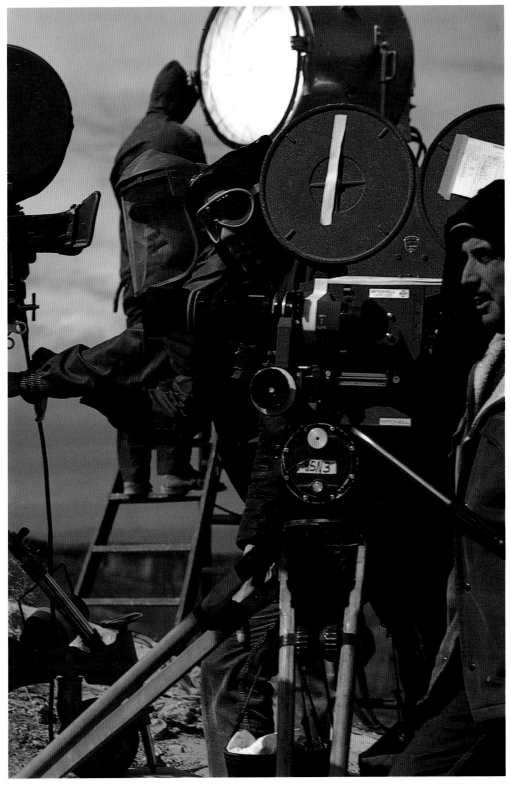

SPAIN
A camera crew shoots a war scene for *Patton*

UNITED STATES
A prop man on the film *The Flight of the Phoenix*

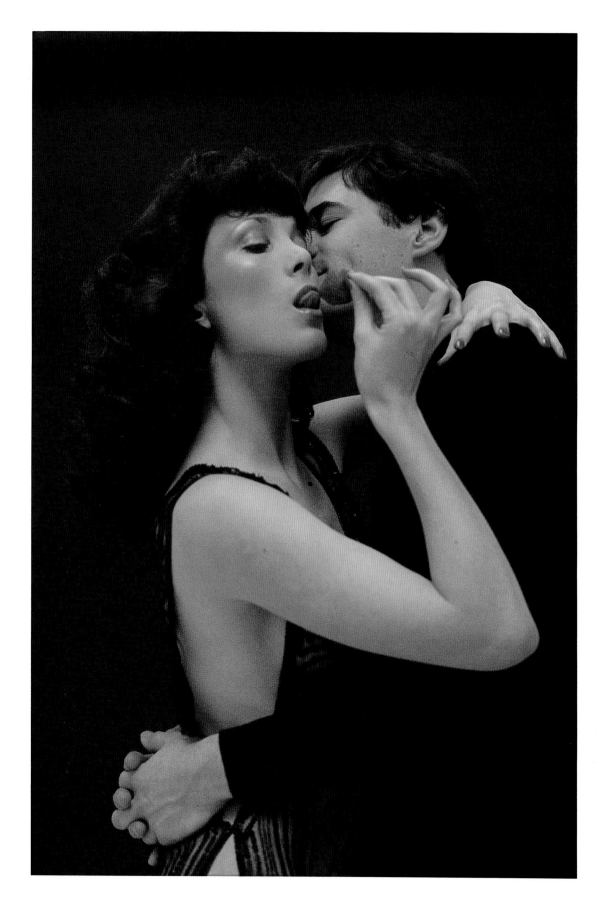

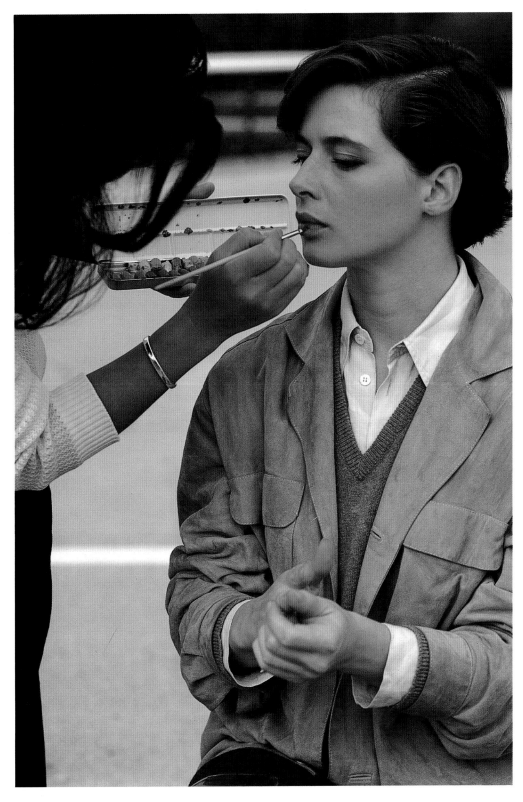

ENGLAND
Models pose for a picture to sell women's hair products

FRANCE
Isabella Rossellini being made up
for a Lancôme advertisement

"It is impossible to enjoy idling thoroughly unless one has plenty of work to do."

—Jerome K. Jerome

India
Yashu, Princess of Gwalior, being dressed for dinner
by her lady-in-waiting

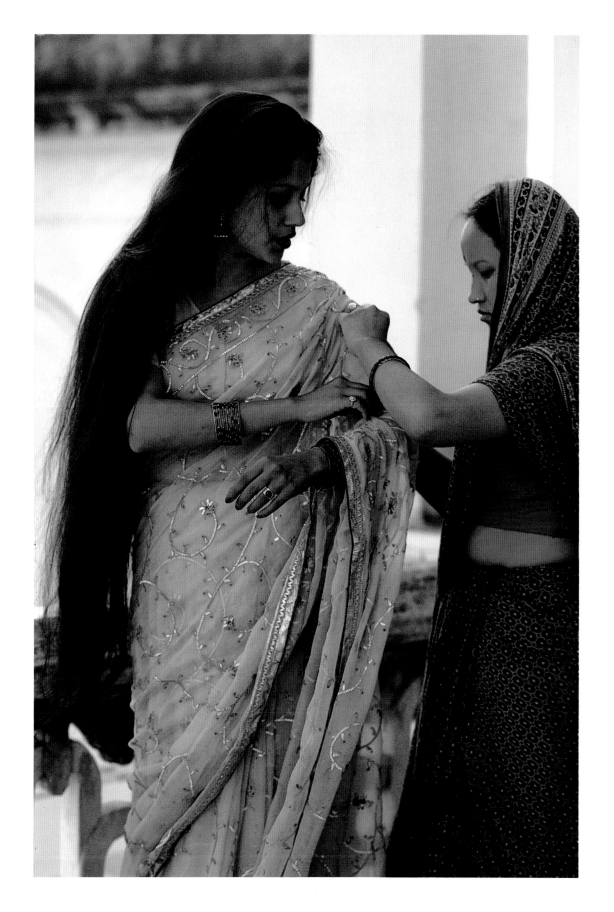

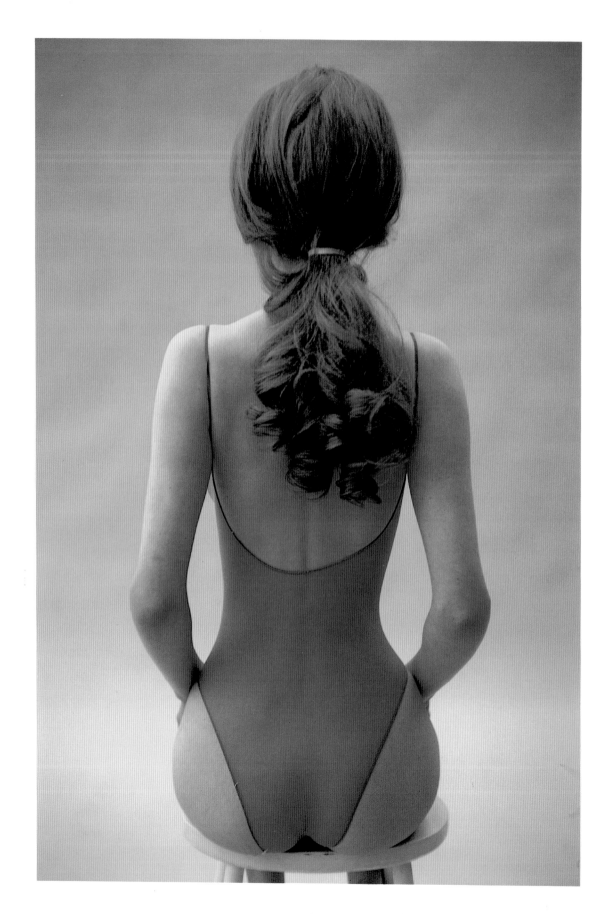

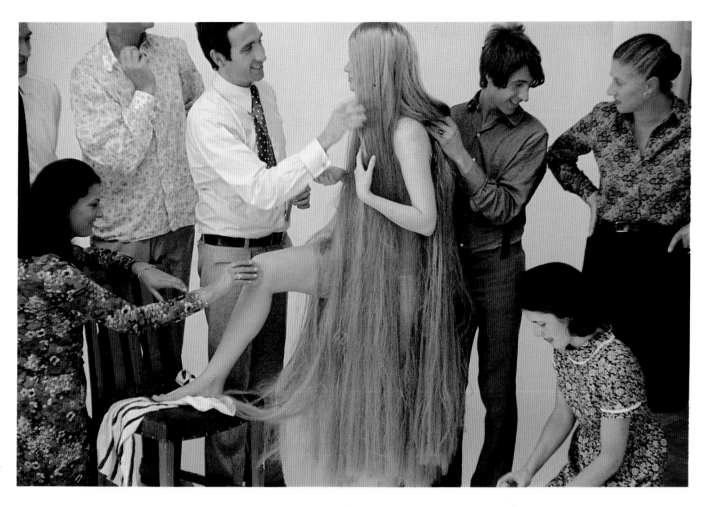

ENGLAND
Preparing a Norman Parkinson photo session for British *Vogue*

ENGLAND
A model poses for an advertisement

63

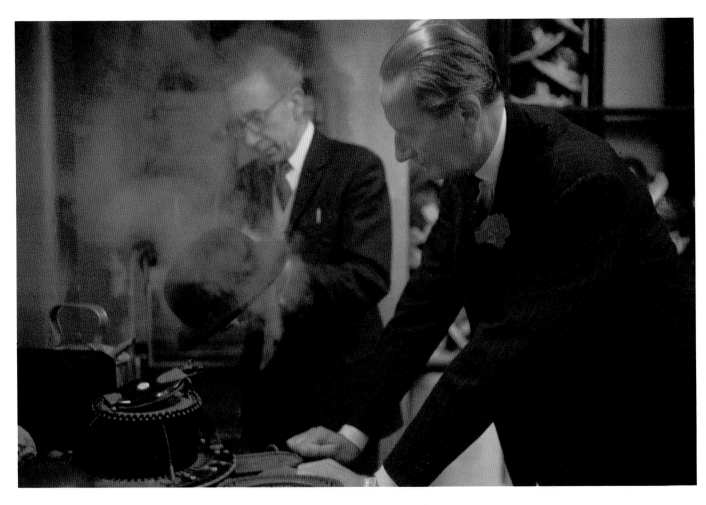

ENGLAND
Blocking a bowler for a "gentleman"

"He that can work is a born king of something."

—Thomas Carlyle

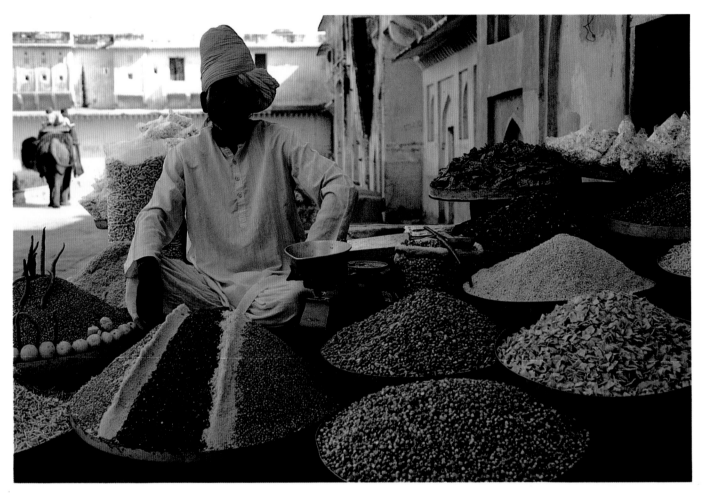

INDIA
Seller of spices and aromatics

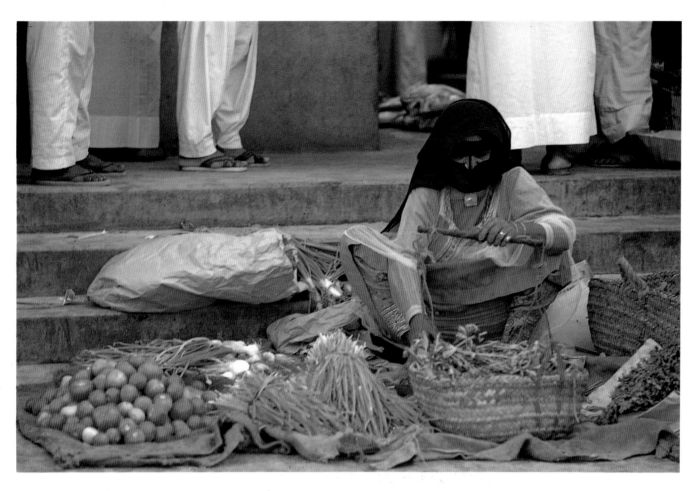

UNITED ARAB EMIRATES
A vegetable seller

"No task, rightly done, is truly private. It is part of the world's work."

—WOODROW WILSON

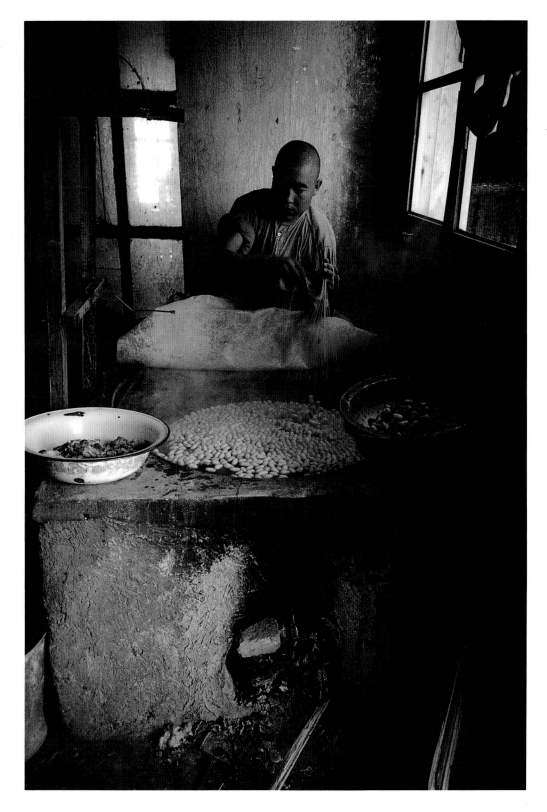

Afghanistan
Removing the strands of silk from heated cocoons

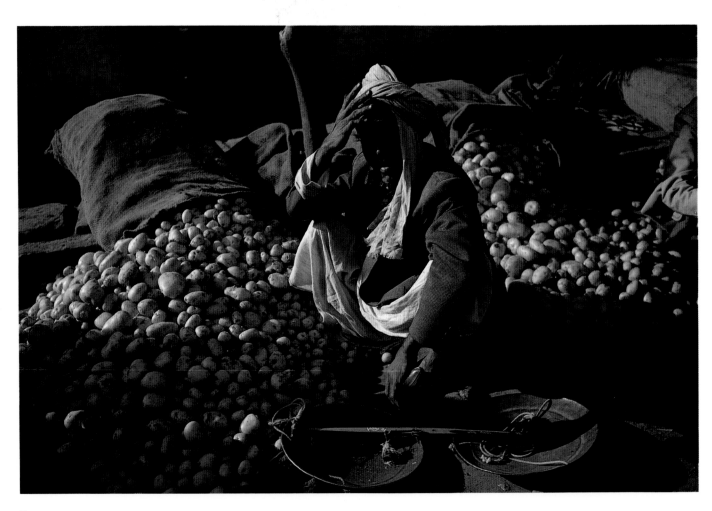

PAKISTAN
Selling potatoes in the marketplace

INDIA
A pepper seller in the market

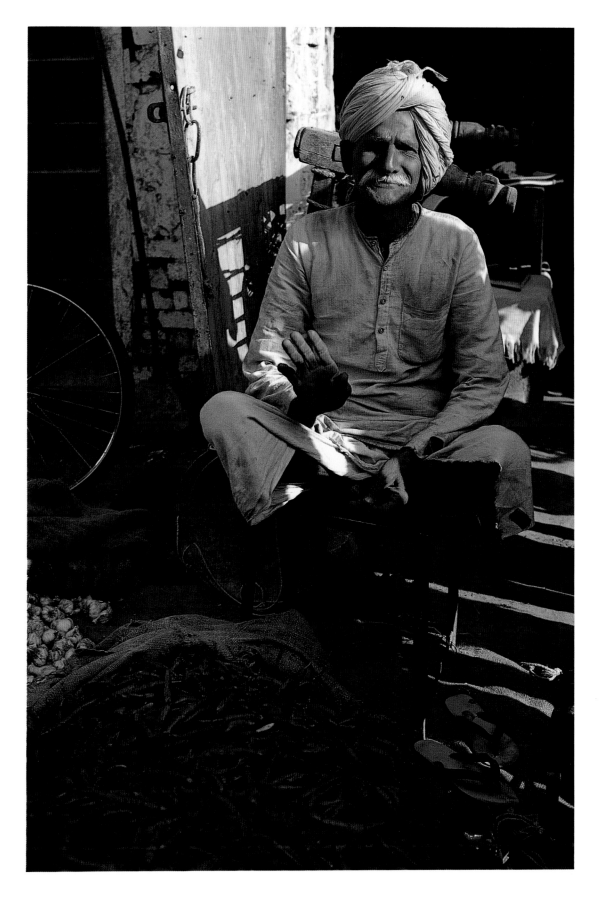

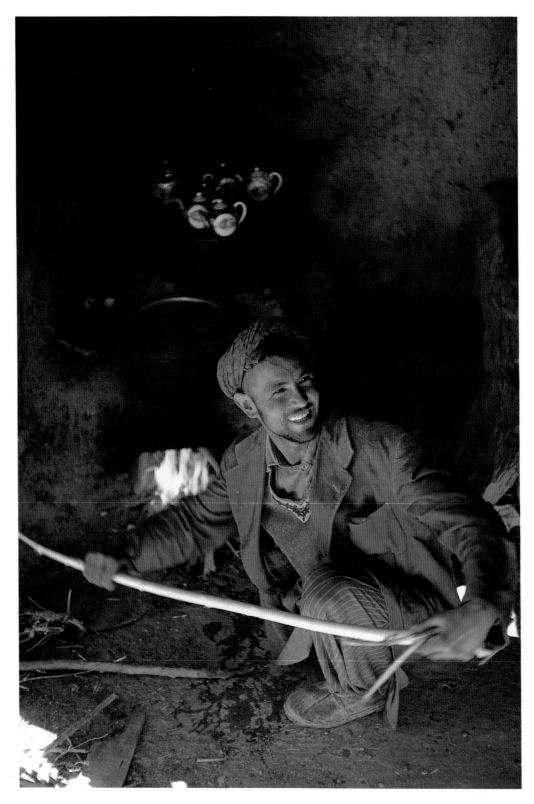

AFGHANISTAN
The tea boy prepares hot water in a tea house

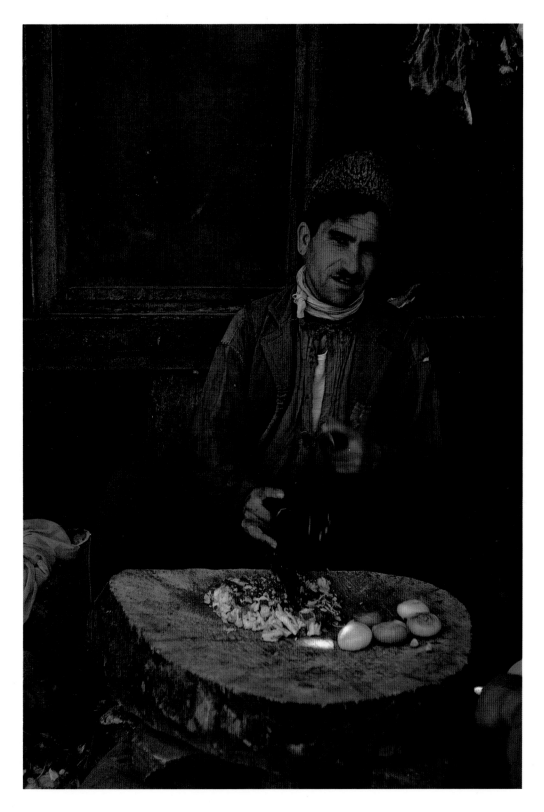

Afghanistan
Hamburger butcher adds an onion to the mixture

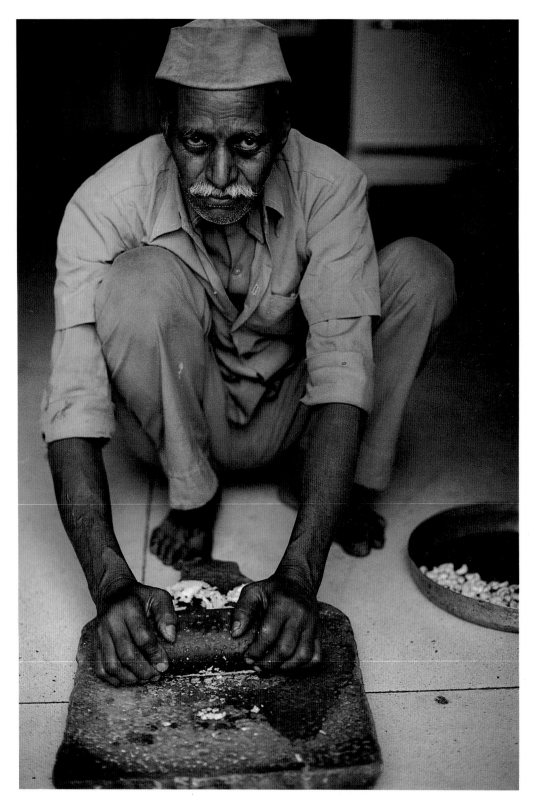

INDIA
Spice blender for curries in the household of the
Maharani of Gwalior

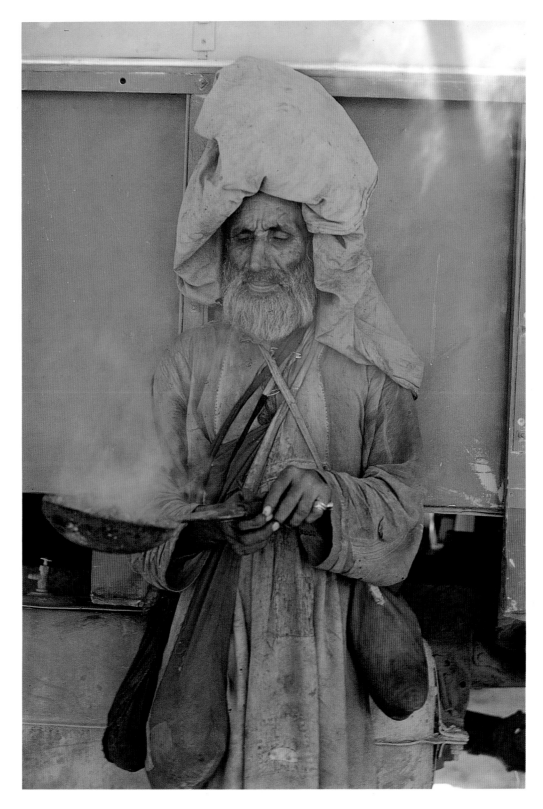

AFGHANISTAN
Every springtime the fumigator goes from house to
house, chasing away evil spirits

"No race can prosper till it learns there is as much dignity in tilling a field as in writing a poem."

—BOOKER T. WASHINGTON

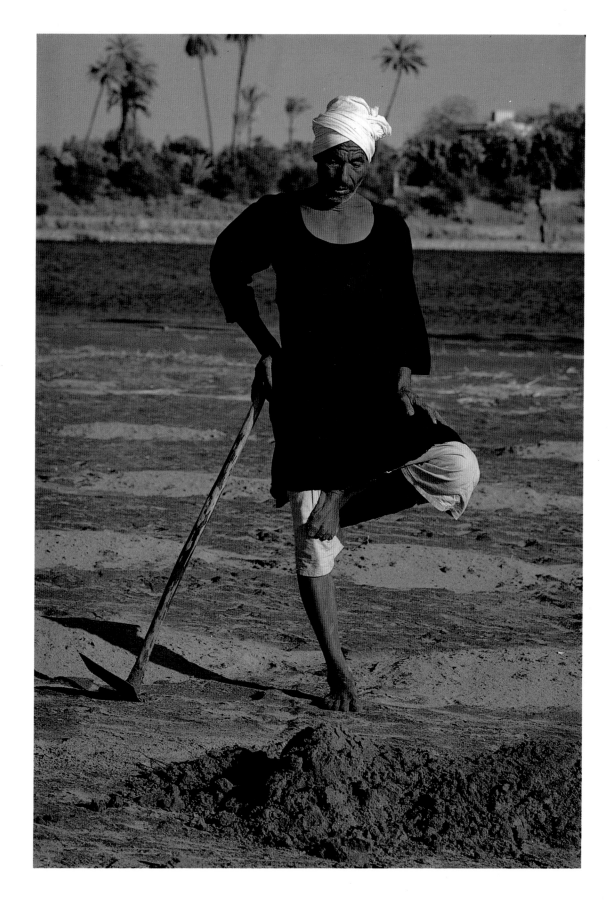

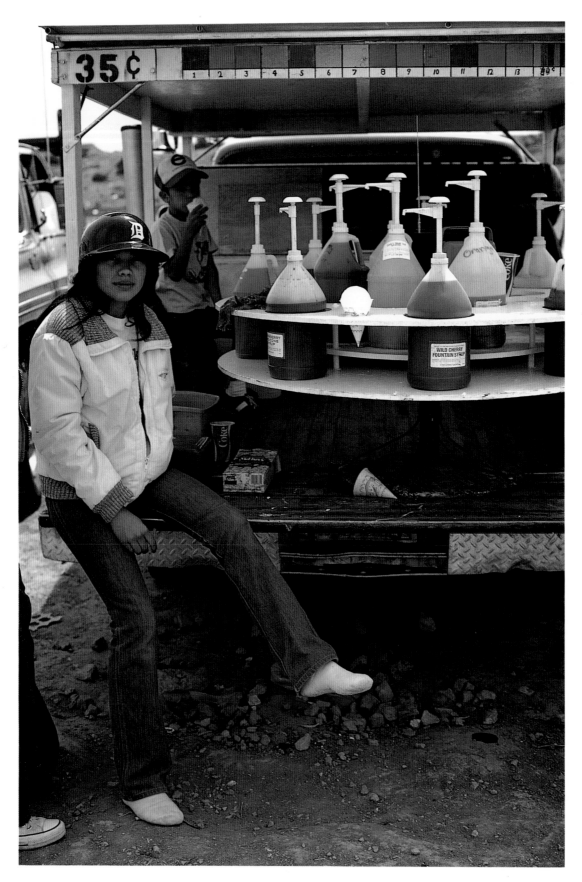

UNITED STATES
Selling syrup over ice shavings on an Indian reservation in New Mexico

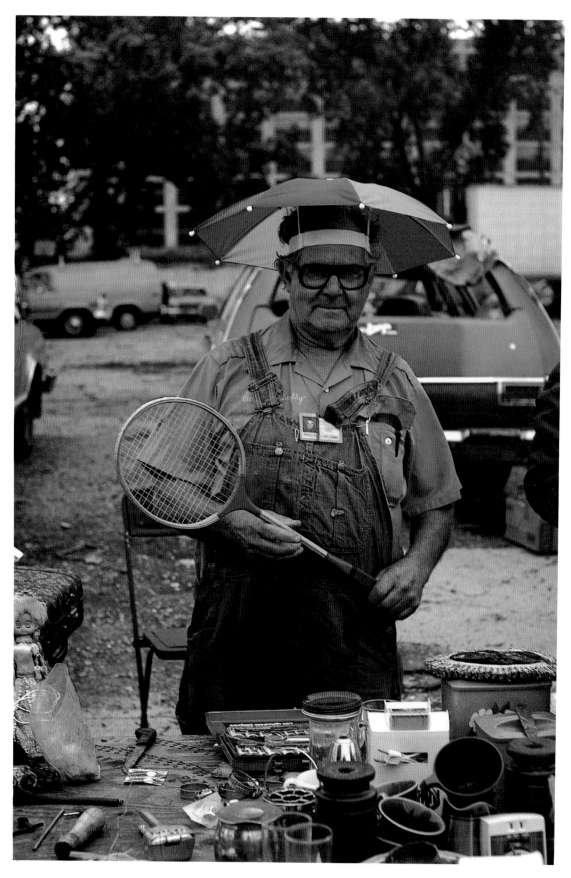

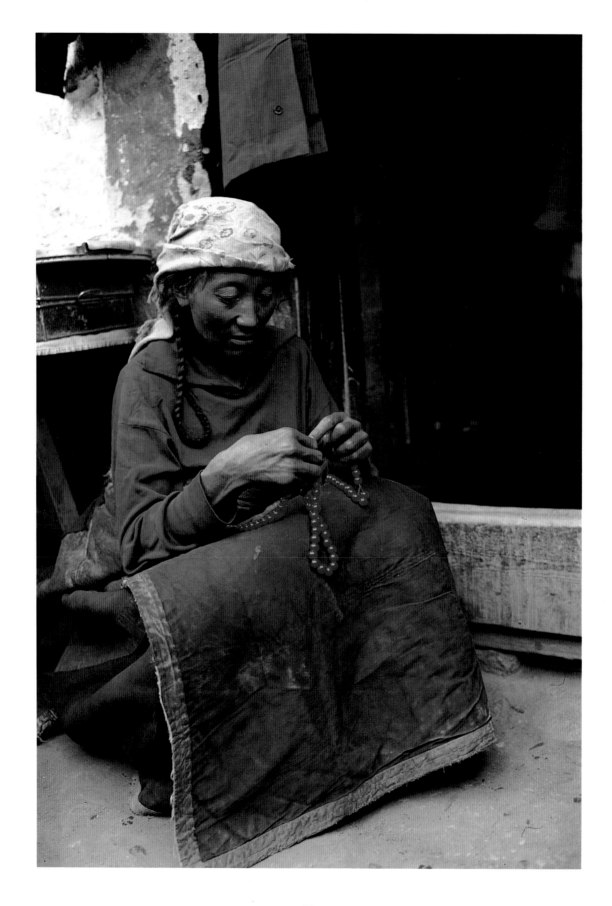

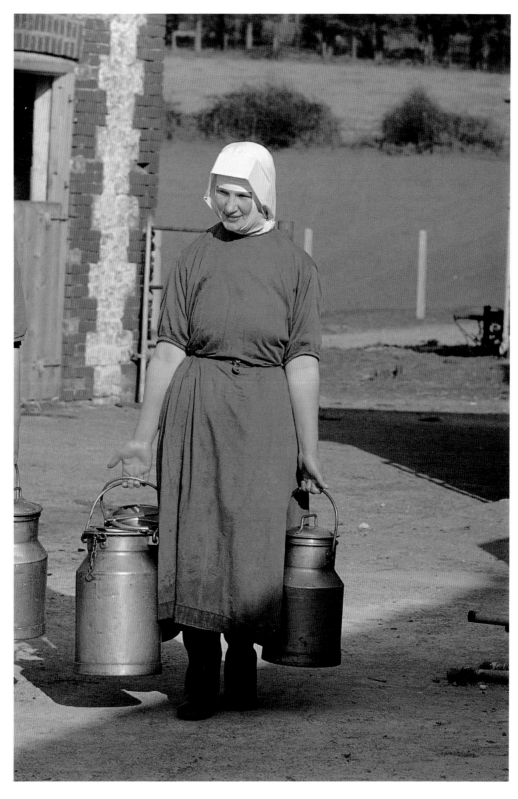

TIBET
Stringing beads

ENGLAND
Novitiate nun as milkmaid

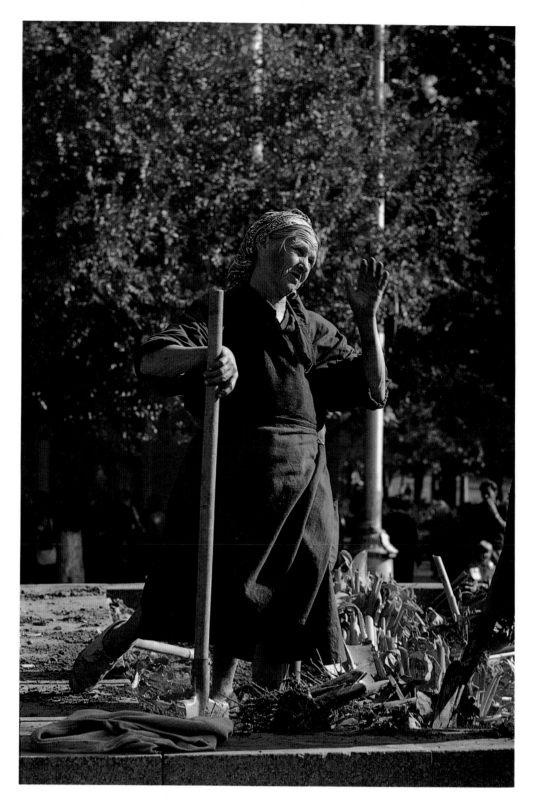

U.S.S.R.
A *babushka* sweeping up the dust of Asia

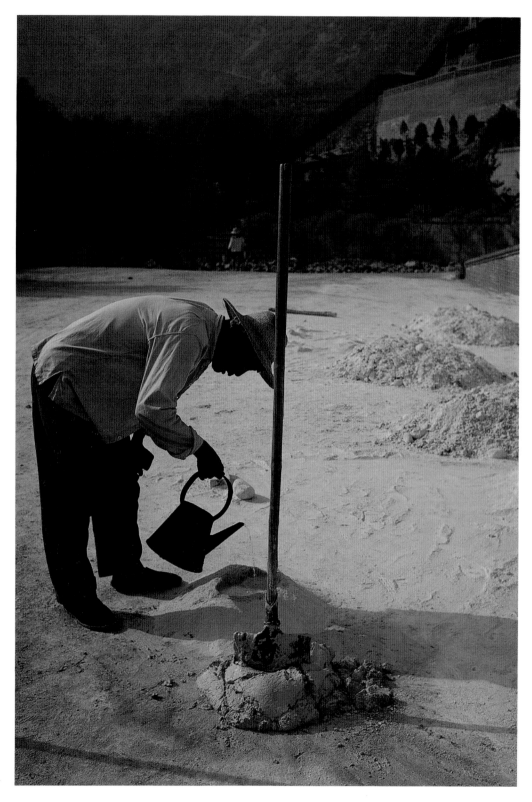

CHINA
Mixing cement

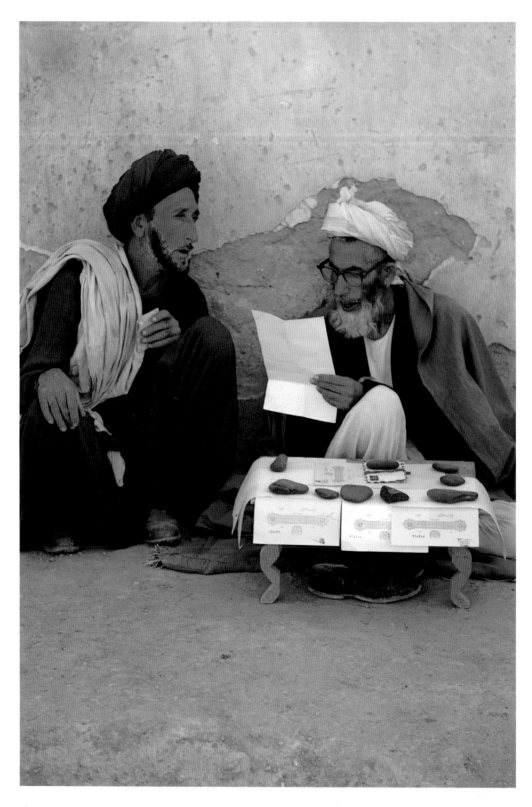

AFGHANISTAN
The village scribe takes dictation from an illiterate
customer

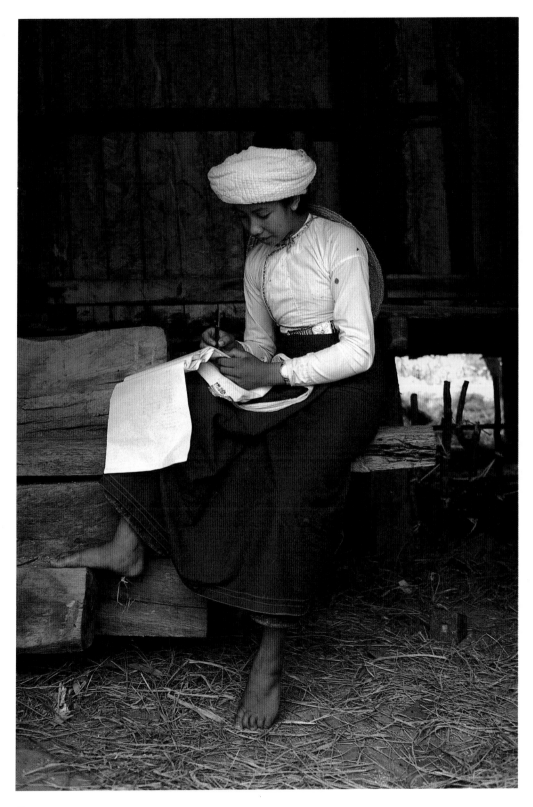

CHINA
Keeping records for the wheat harvest

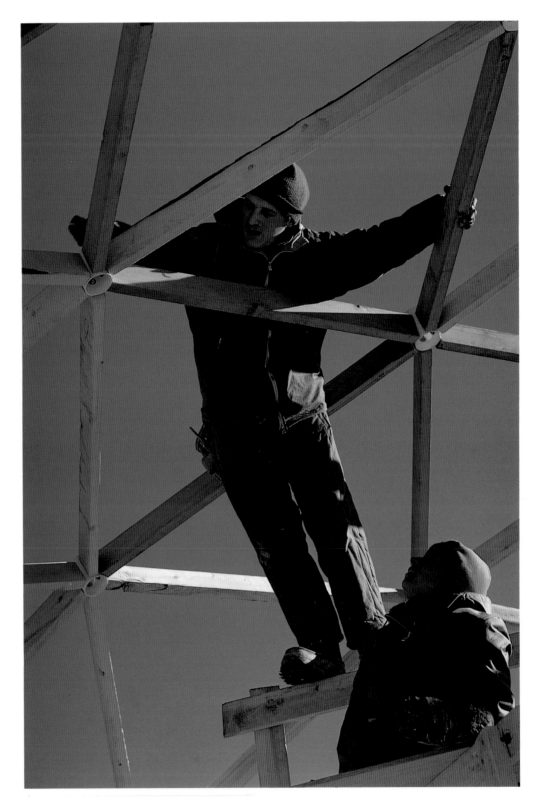

UNITED STATES
Artists build a communal geodesic-dome studio in the Rockies

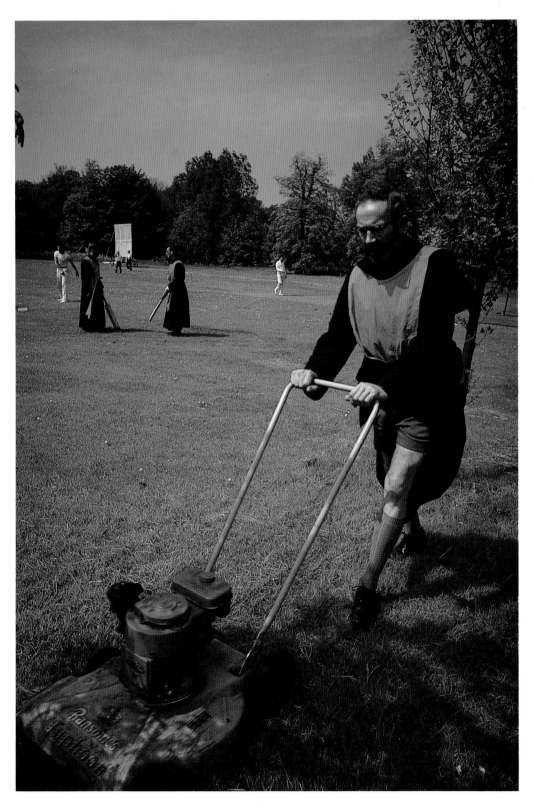

A monk mows the monastery lawn

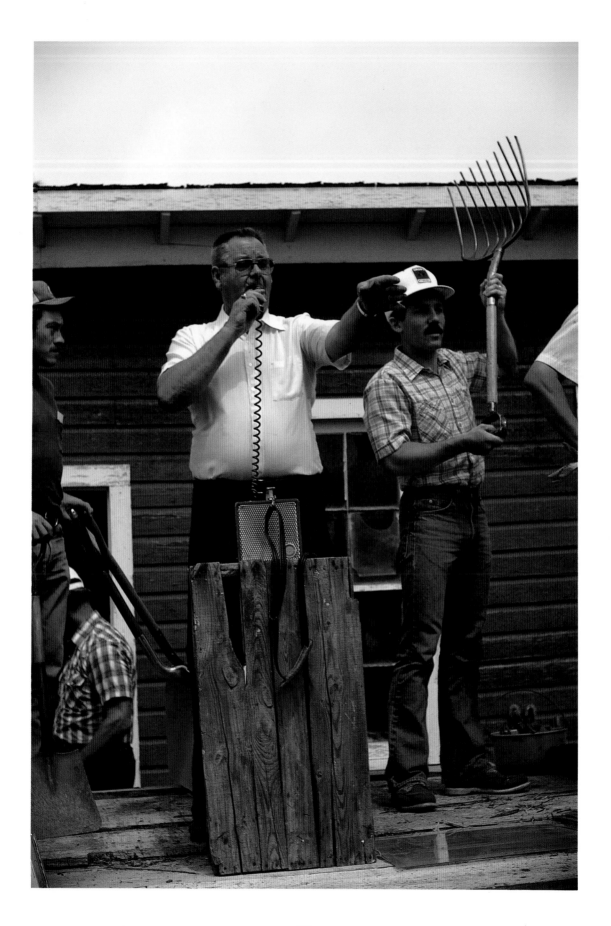

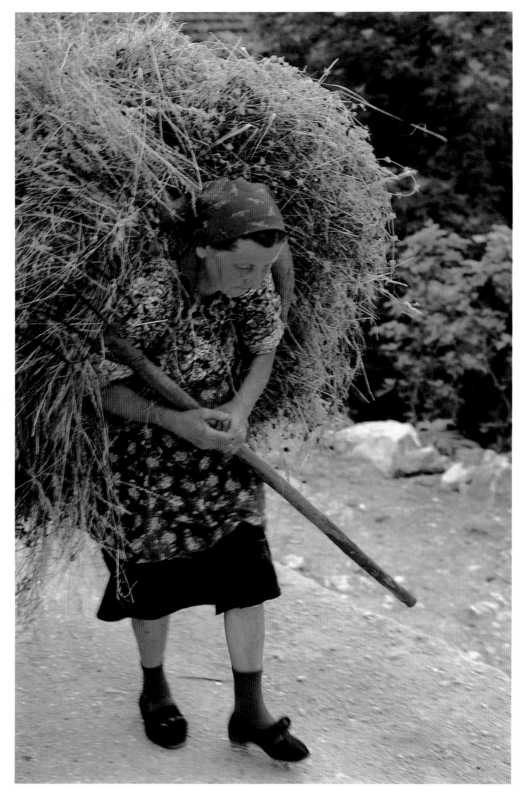

YUGOSLAVIA
A farmer's wife

UNITED STATES
Implements are auctioned at a farm foreclosure in Nebraska

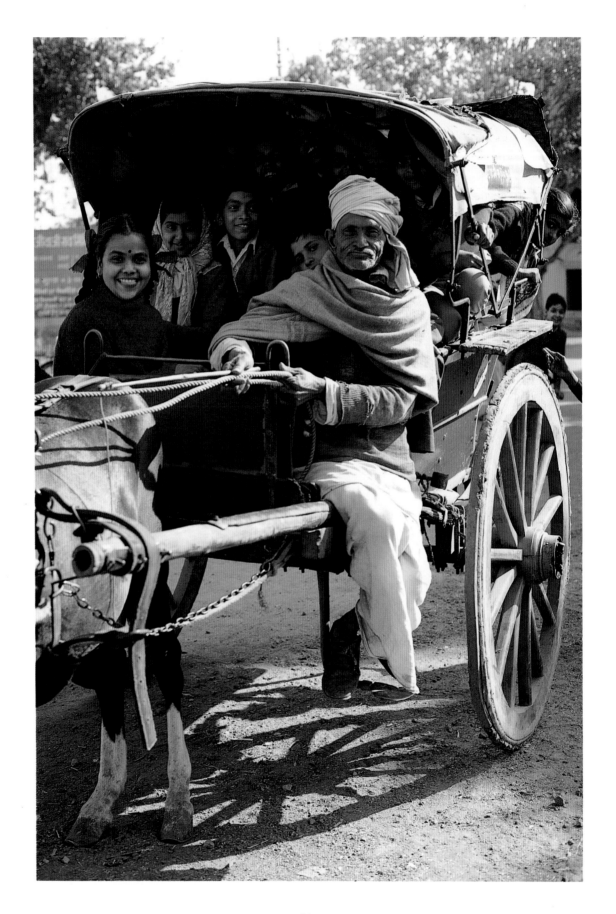

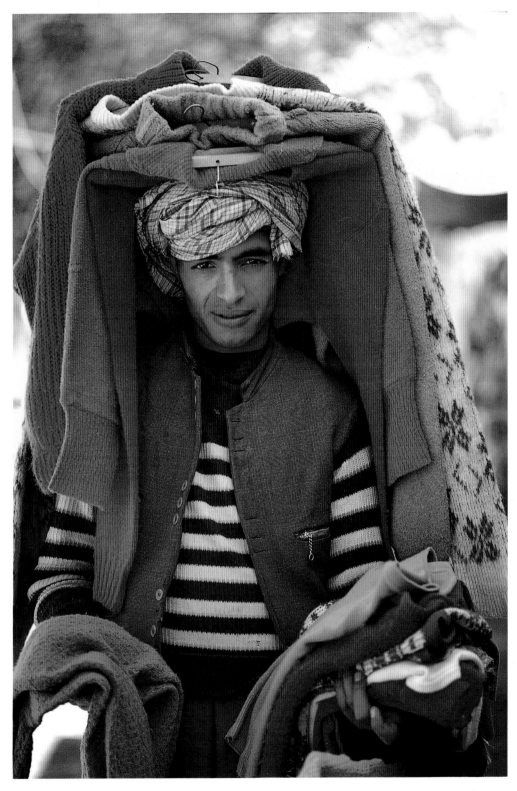

INDIA
The local school bus of Gwalior

AFGHANISTAN
A peddler carries his wares on his back

OVERLEAF: UNITED ARAB EMIRATES
A truckload of new labor recruits from Iran

91

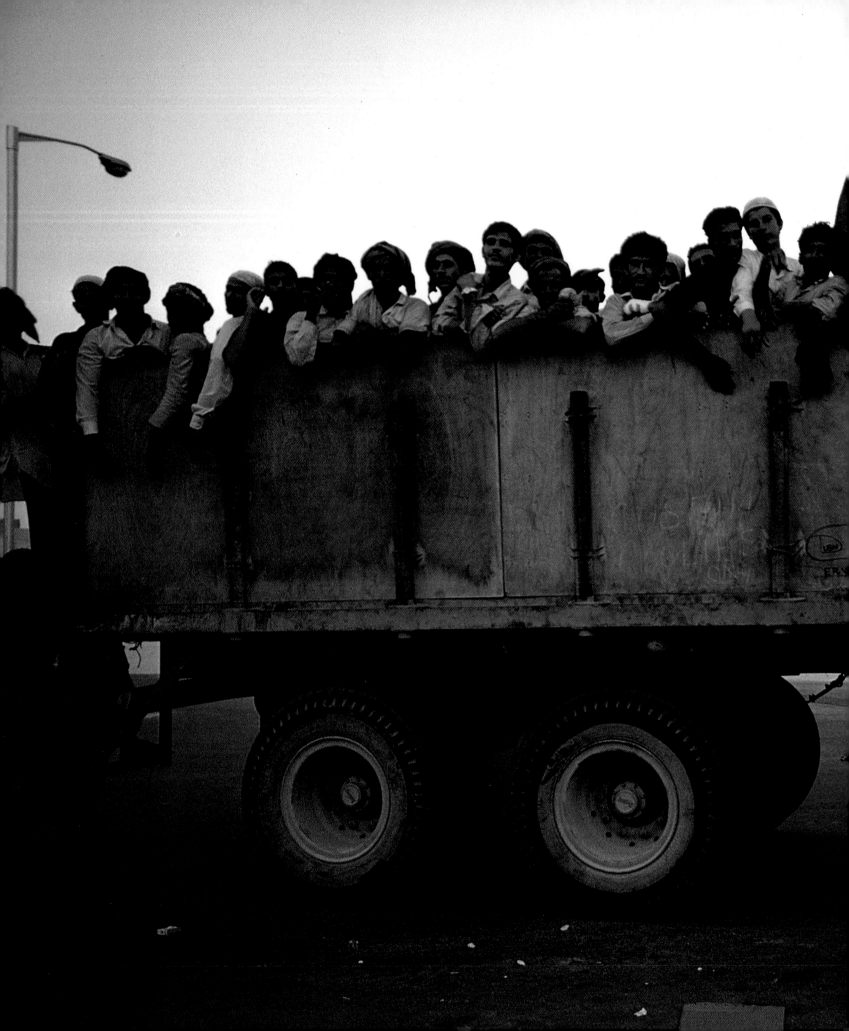

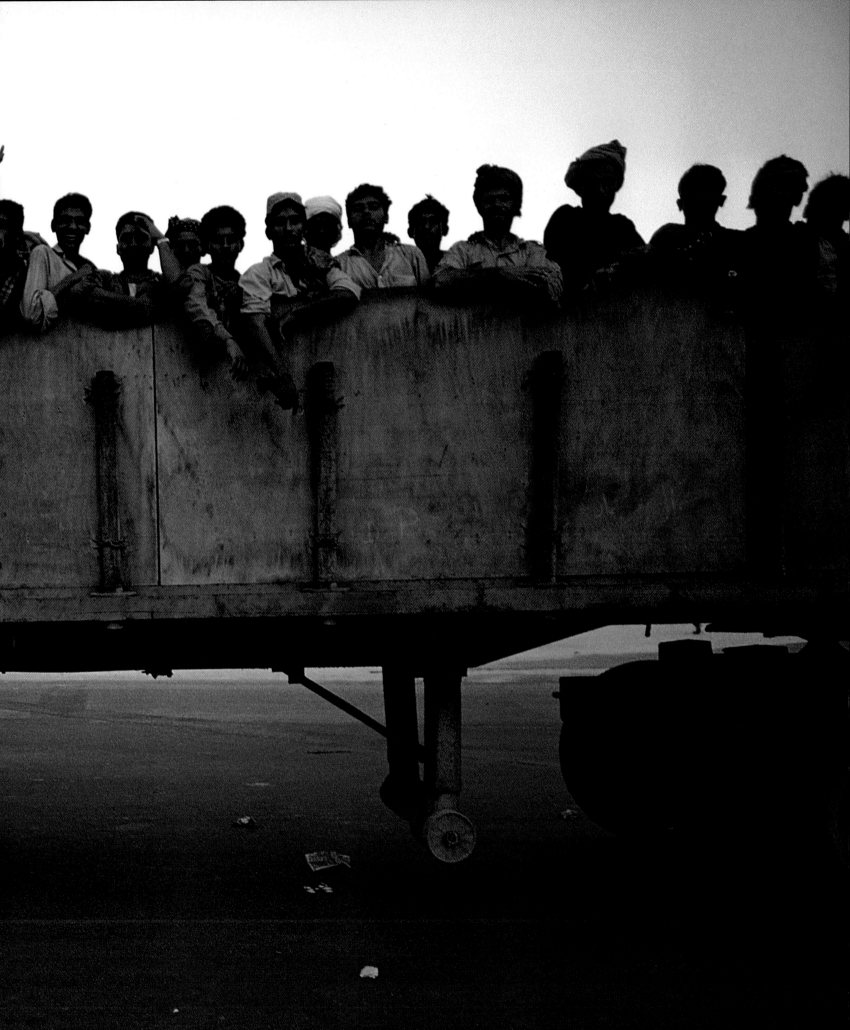

"Don't condescend to unskilled labor. Try it for half a day first."

—BROOKS ATKINSON

AFGHANISTAN
Human labor is cheaper than animal labor or machinery

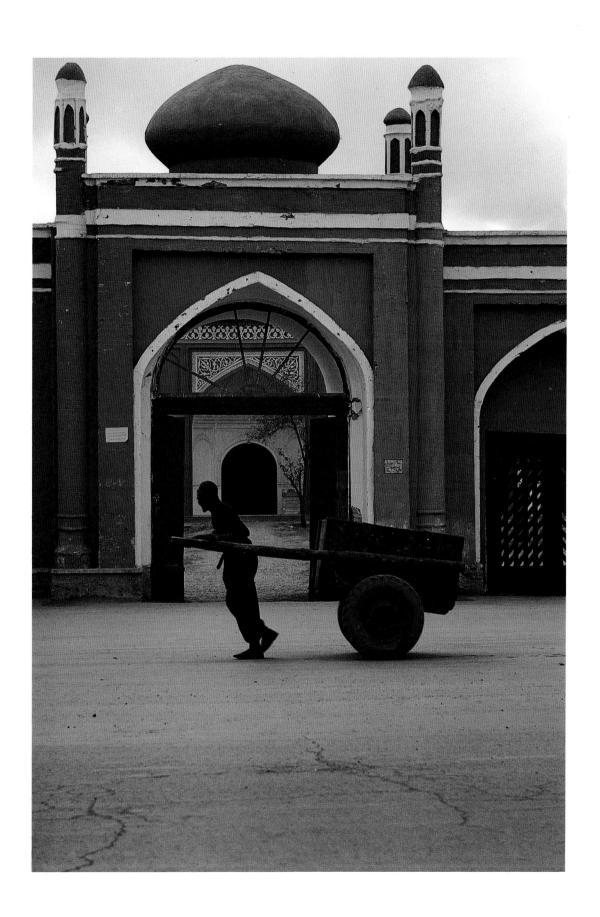

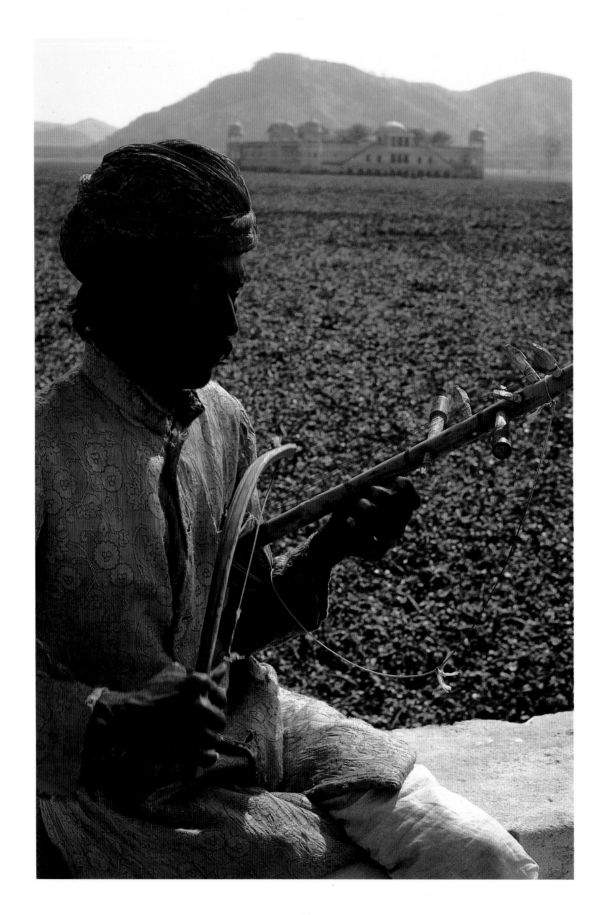

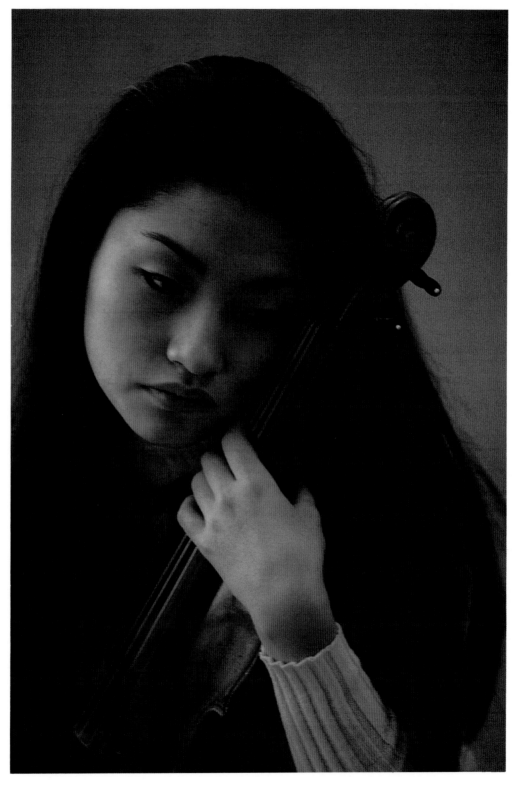

ENGLAND
Kyung Wha Chung before a concert

INDIA
Itinerant musician for hire

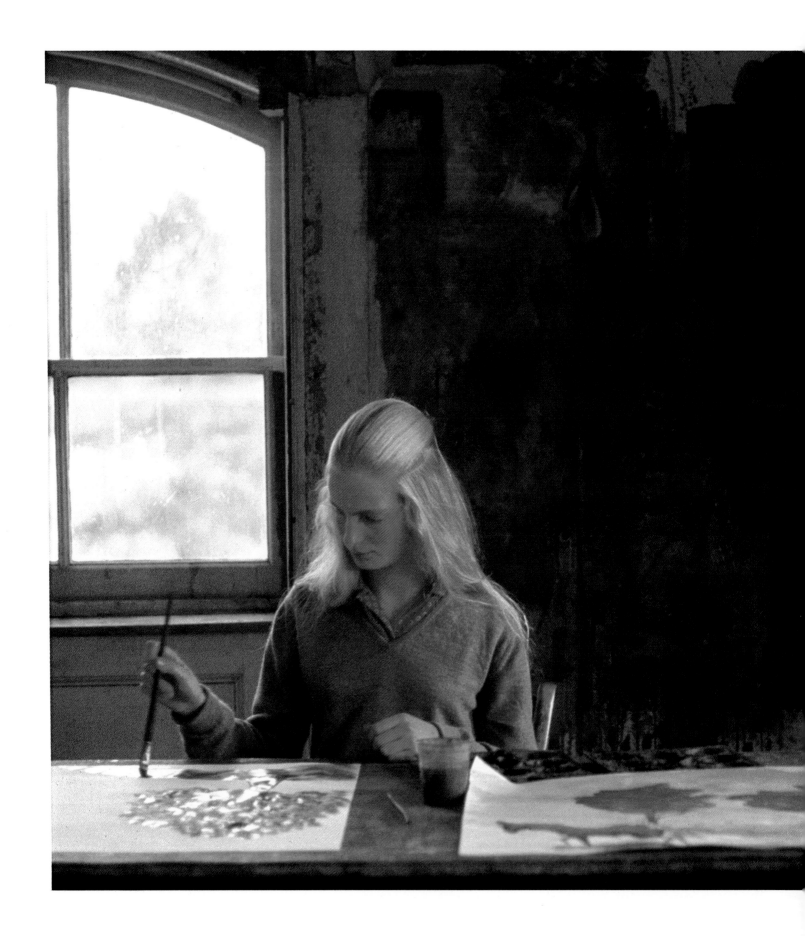

ENGLAND
An art student paints a picture for a school exhibition

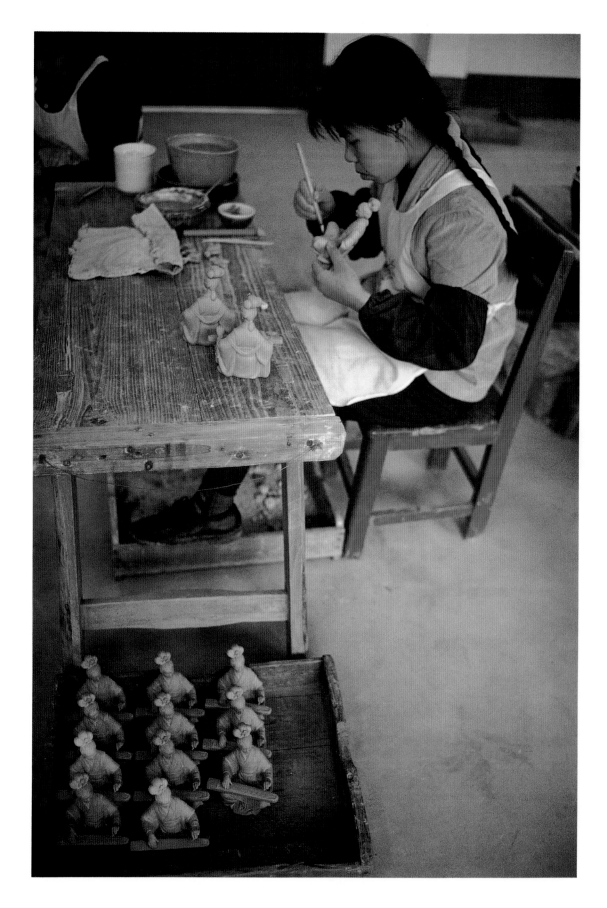

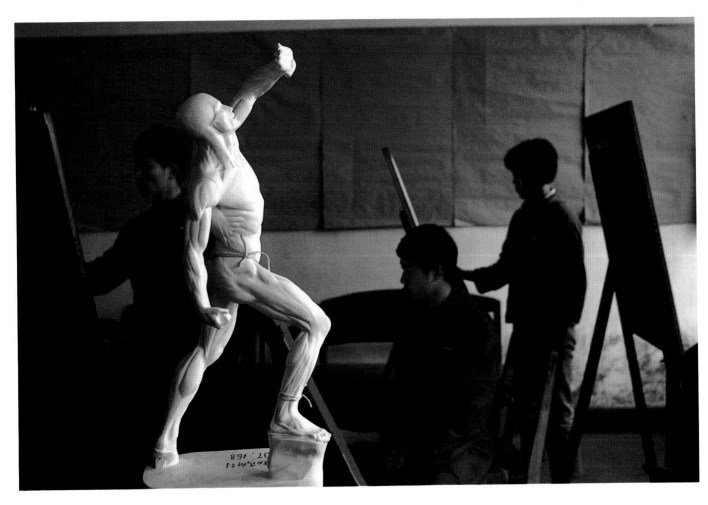

CHINA
A drawing class for trainees in advertising

CHINA
Painting souvenirs

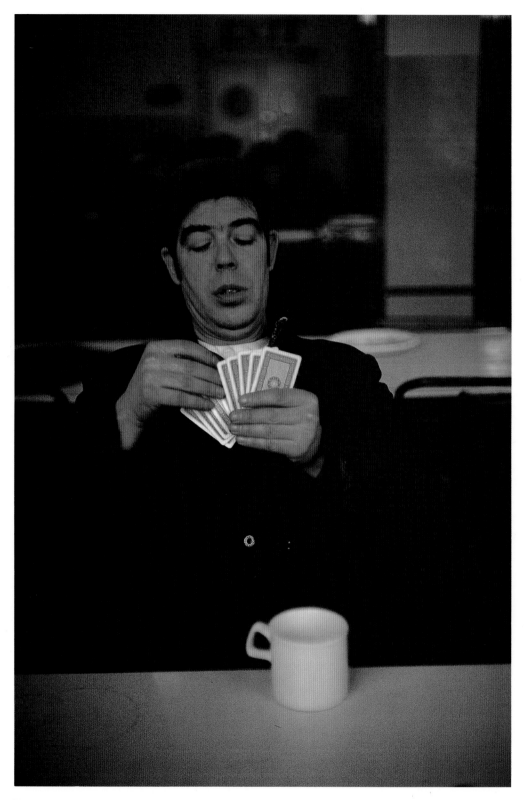

ENGLAND
Lunch break at the workmen's club

ENGLAND
A student in mathematics class at a private girls' school

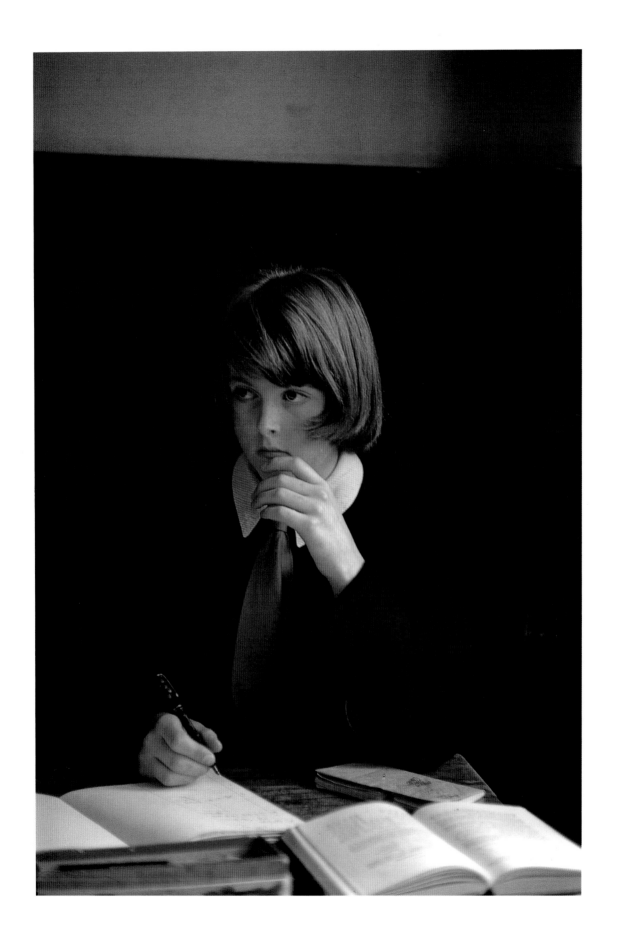

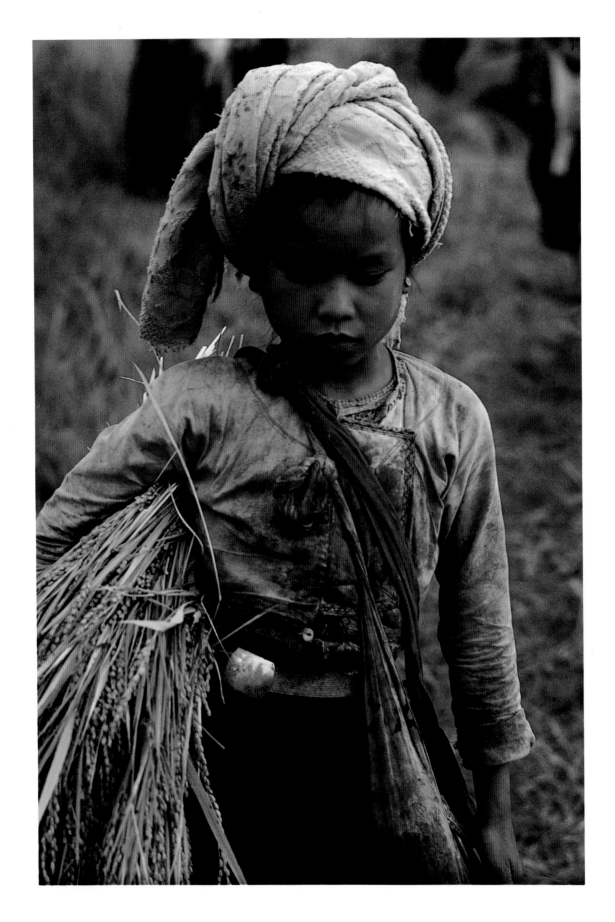

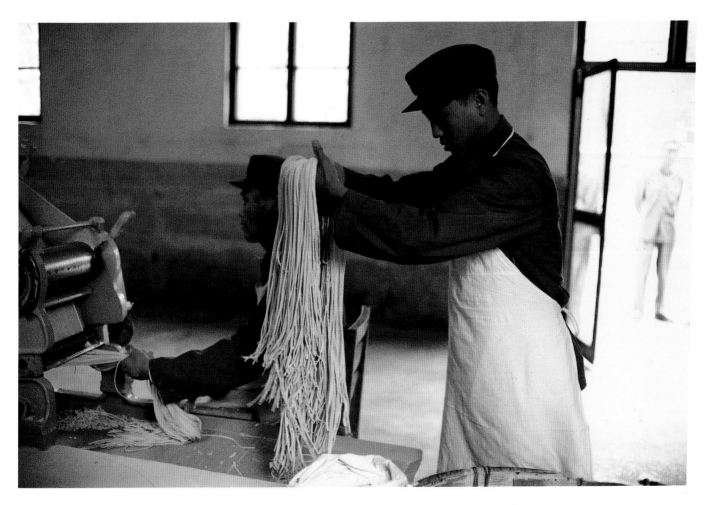

CHINA
A soldier makes noodles for lunch

CHINA
Even the very young help to bring in the harvest

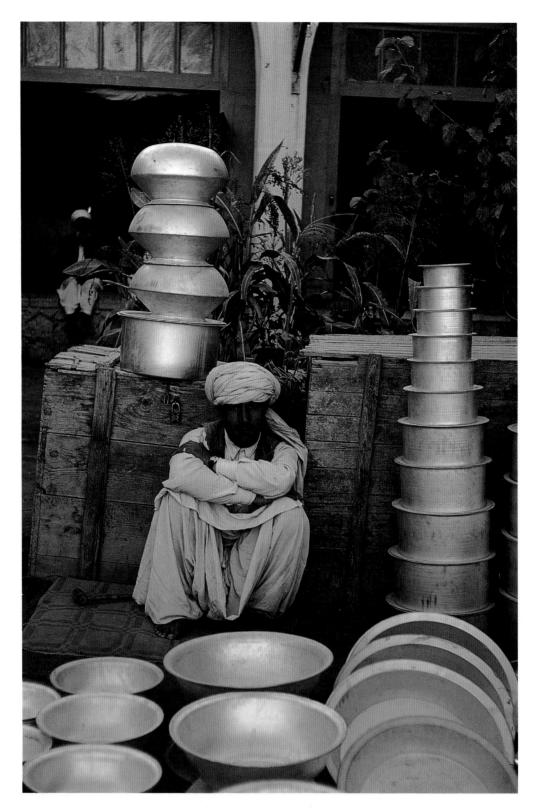

PAKISTAN
Selling tin pots in the *souk*

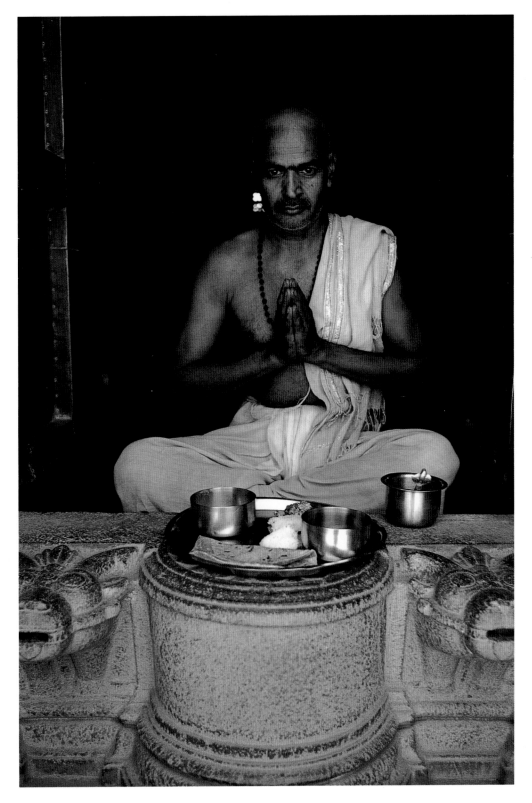

INDIA
A Brahmin priest blesses the food for an ancestor long dead

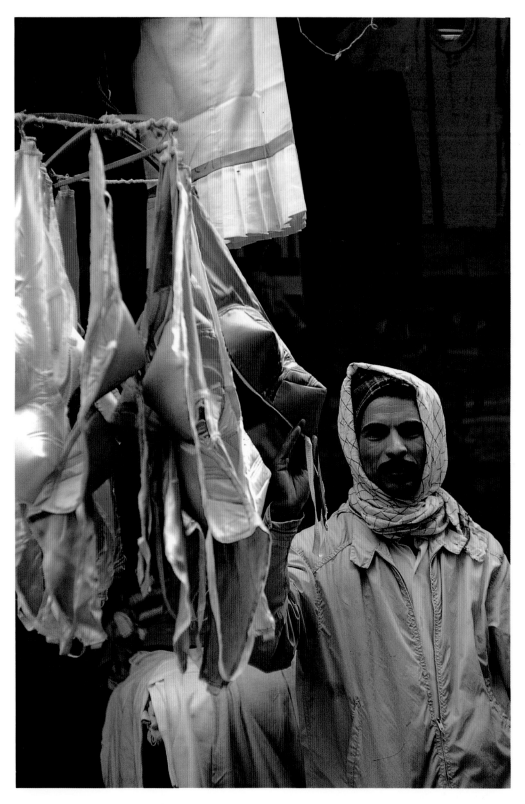

EGYPT
A pushcart vendor peddling his wares

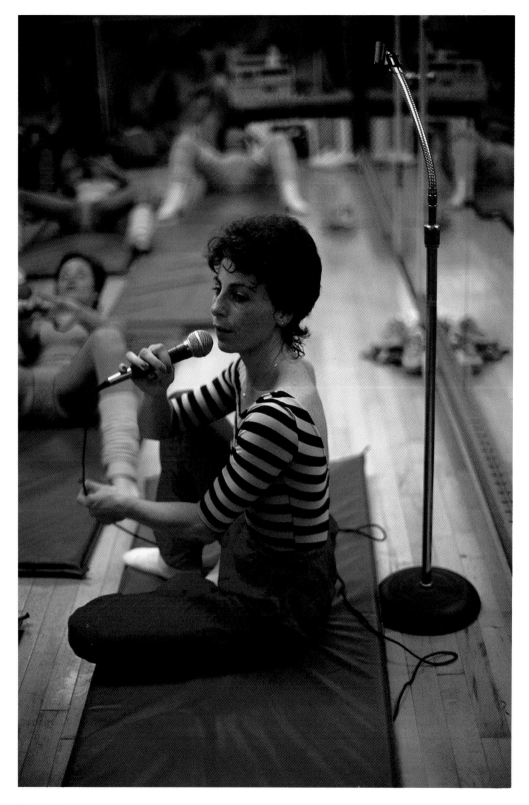

UNITED STATES
An exercise class receives instructions

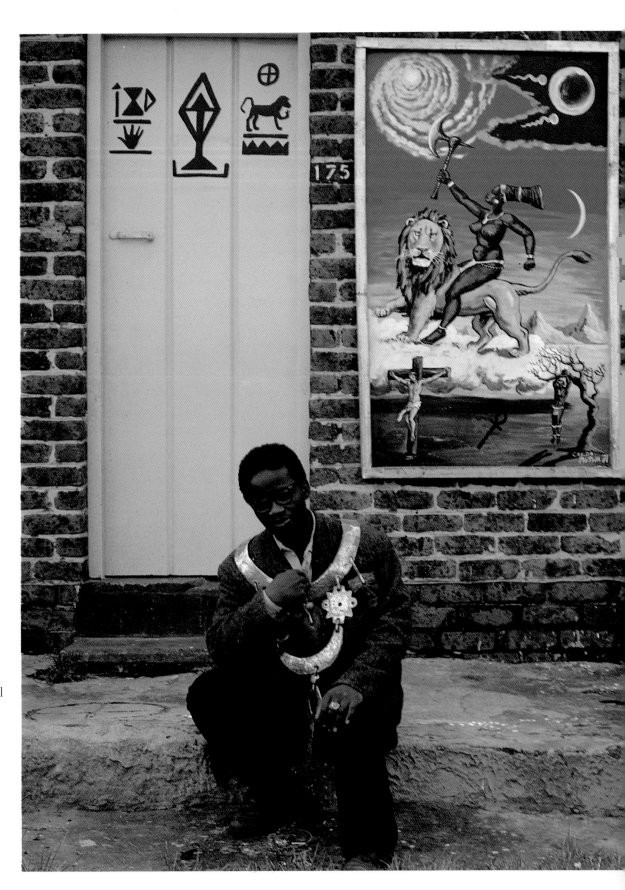

SOUTH AFRICA
Witch doctor with exorcism doll

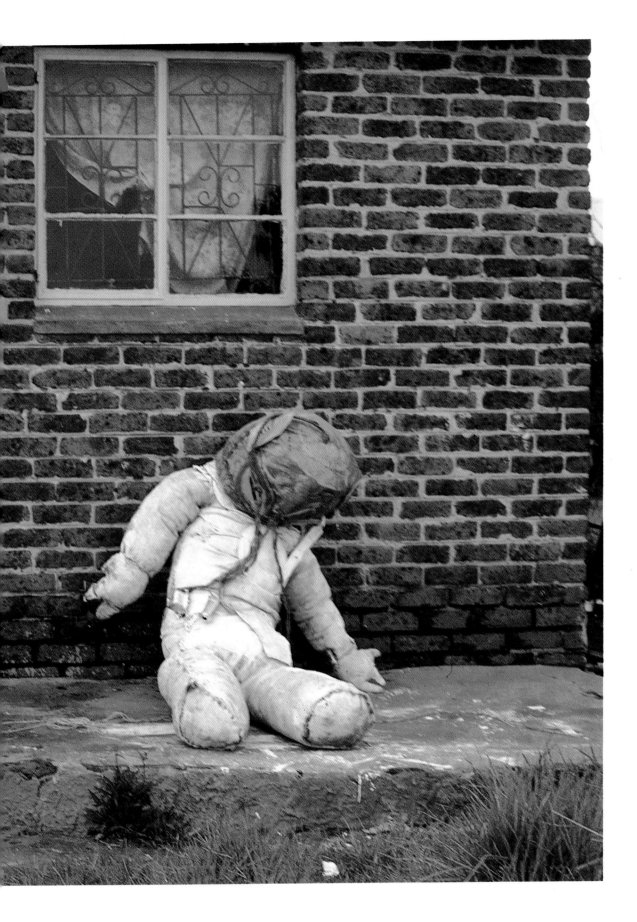

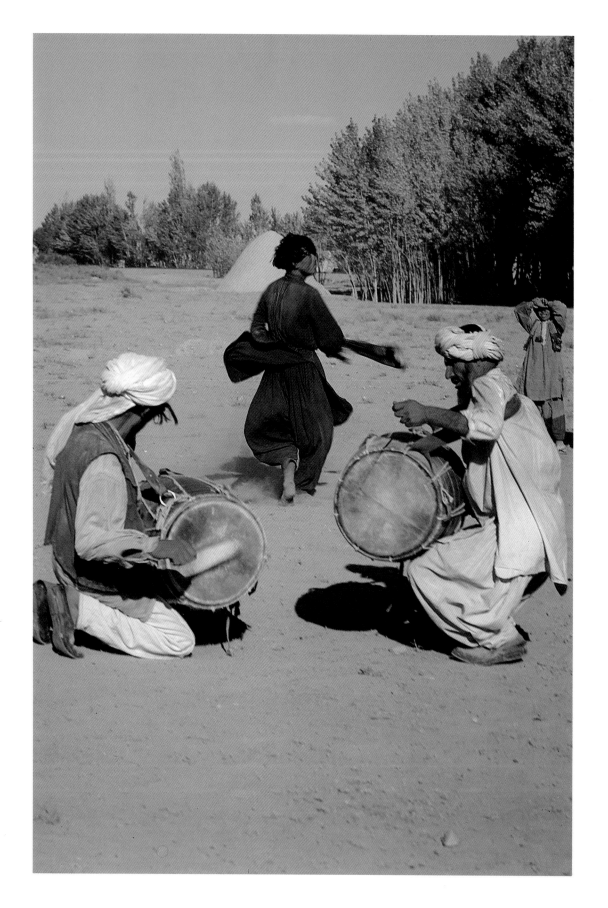

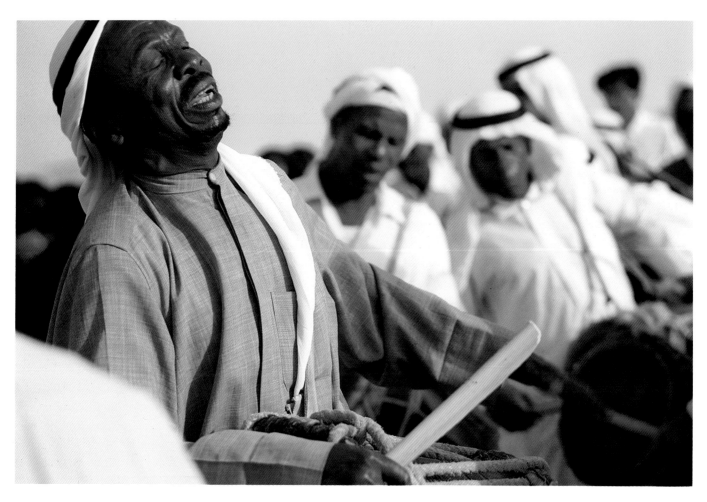

UNITED ARAB EMIRATES
Religious drumming for the wedding of the Crown
Prince of Dubai

AFGHANISTAN
Drummers and dancer in the Hindu Kush on their
way to a nomad wedding

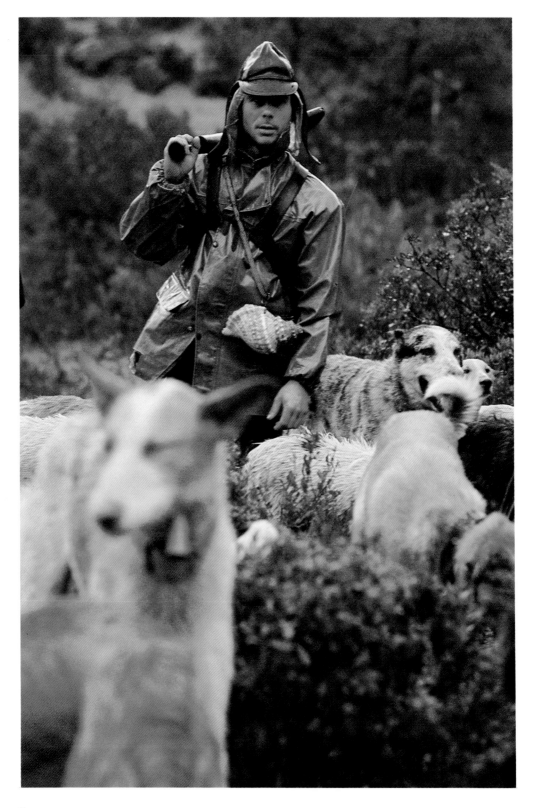

SPAIN
A beater and his dogs on a boar hunt in the Sierra Morena

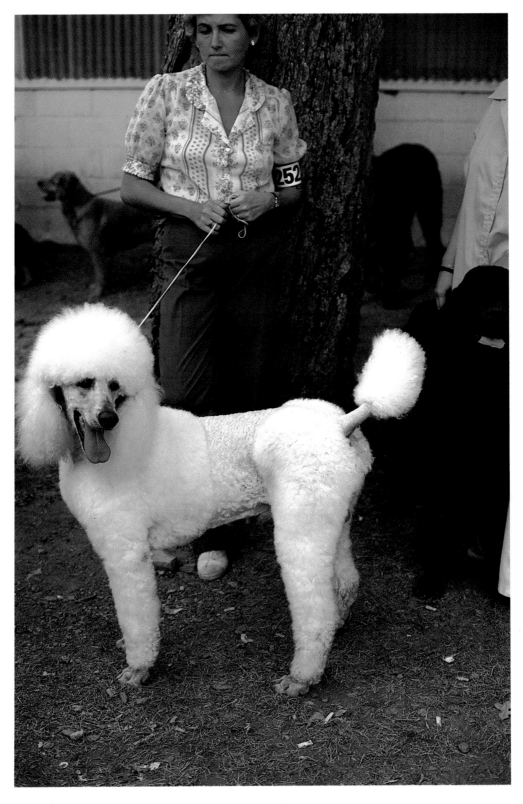

UNITED STATES
A dog show, before the judging begins

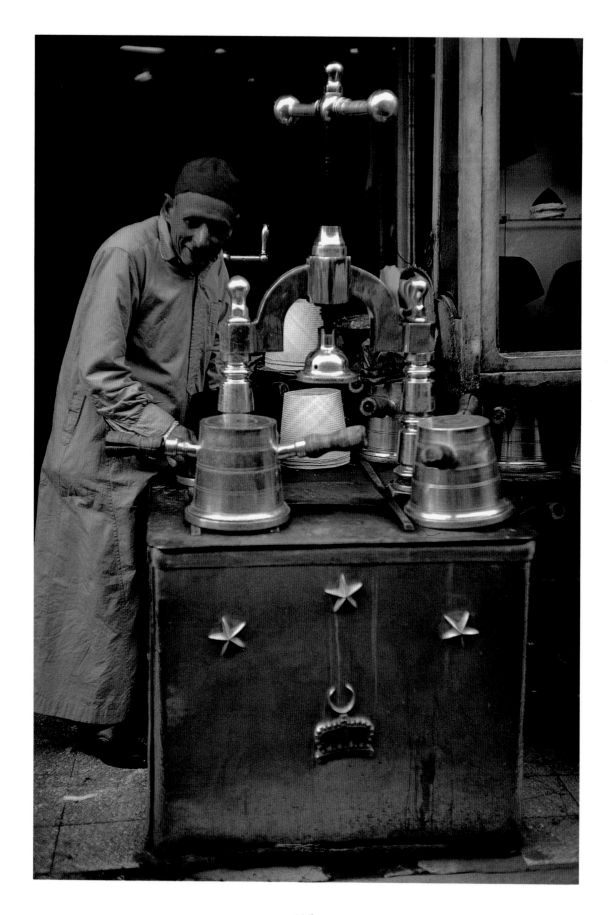

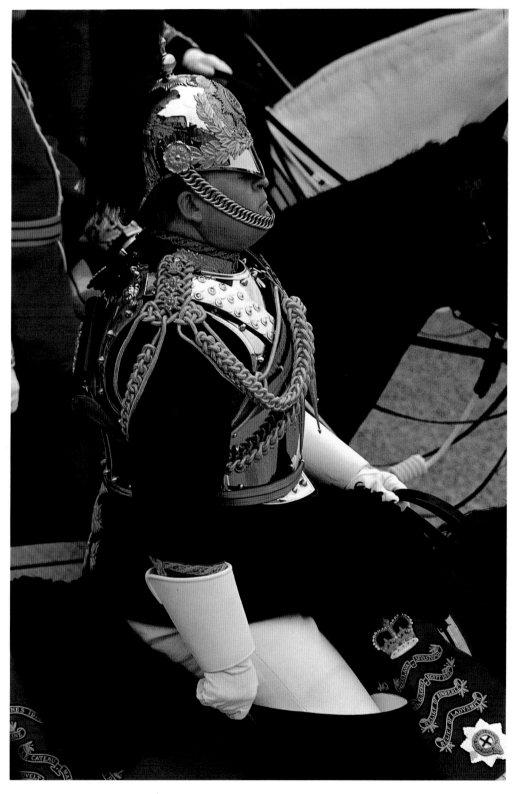

ENGLAND
Preparing for trooping the colors to celebrate
the Queen's birthday

EGYPT
A hatmaker blocking a fez

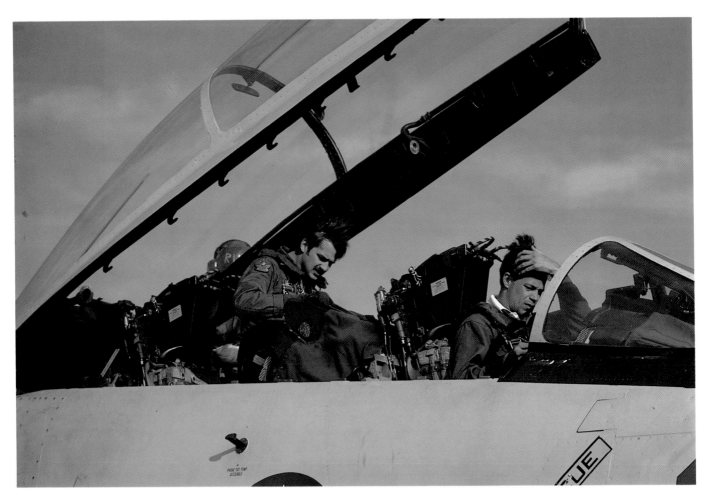

UNITED STATES
A bomber crew about to take off

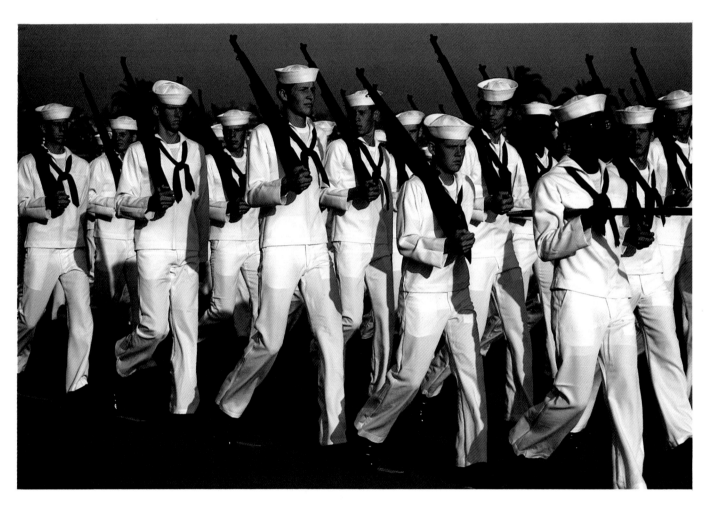

UNITED STATES
Sailors at graduation exercises

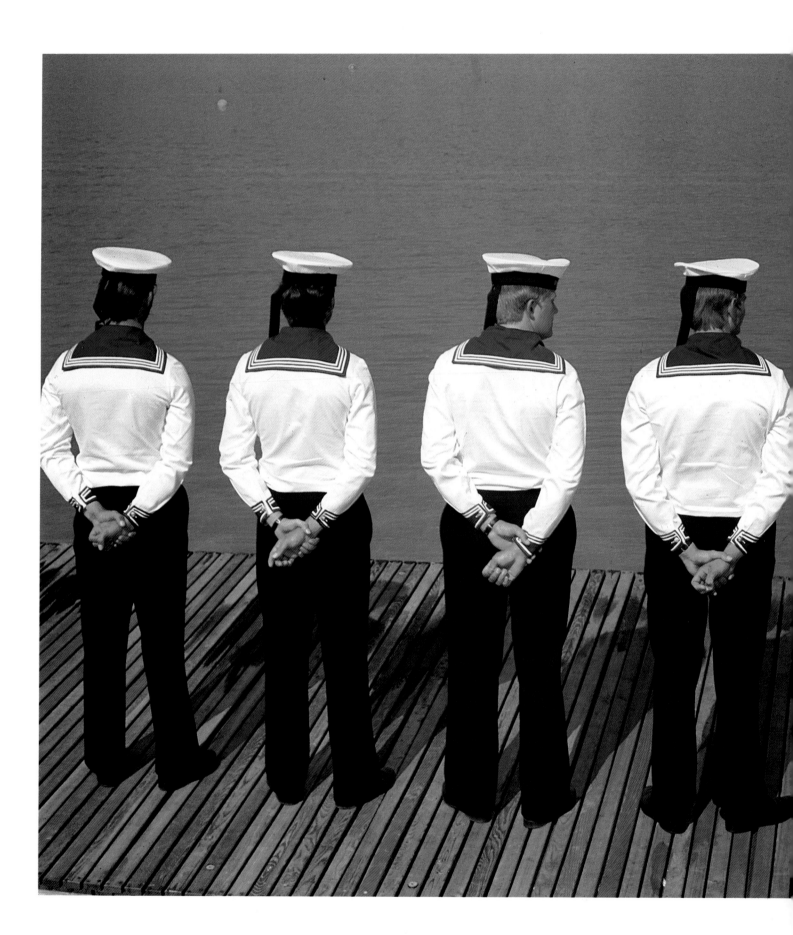

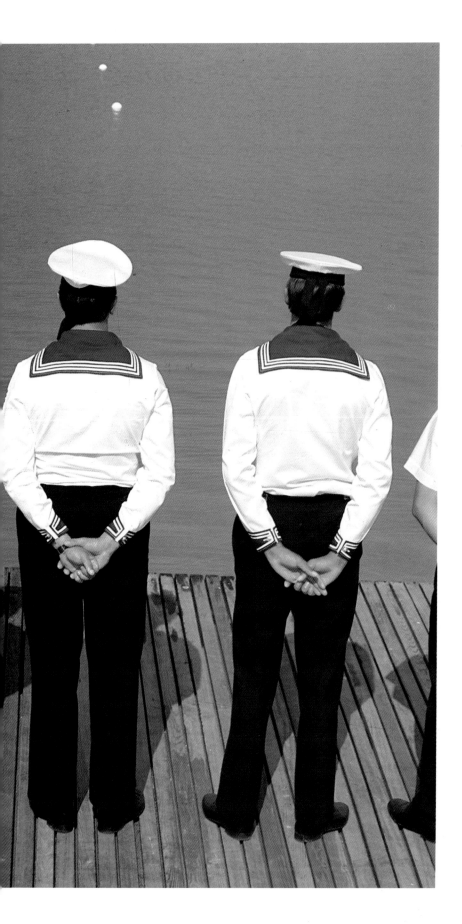

"I like work; it fascinates me. I can sit and look at it for hours. I love to keep it by me: the idea of getting rid of it nearly breaks my heart."

—JEROME K. JEROME

GERMANY
Sailors at a lakeside in Munich

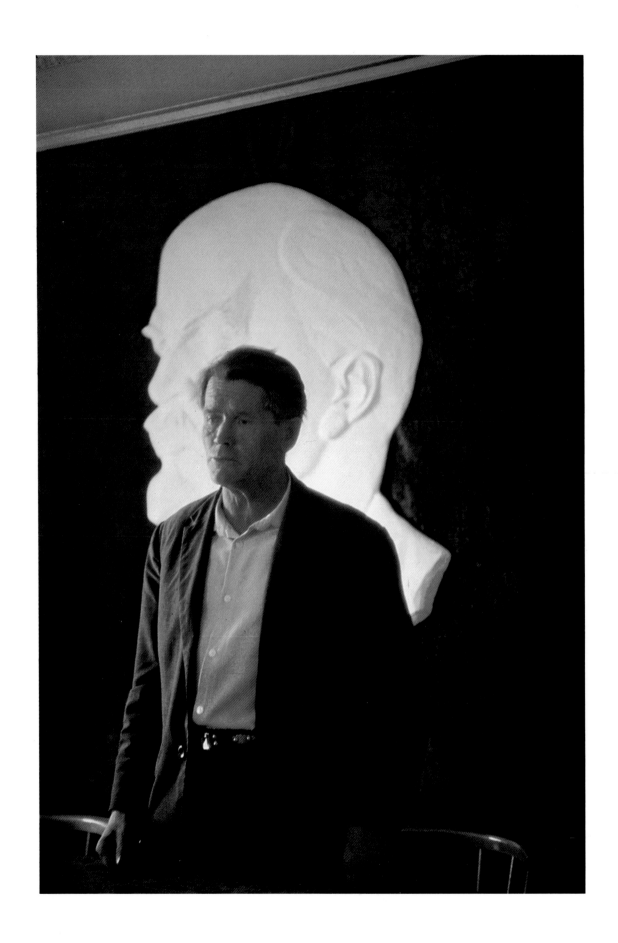

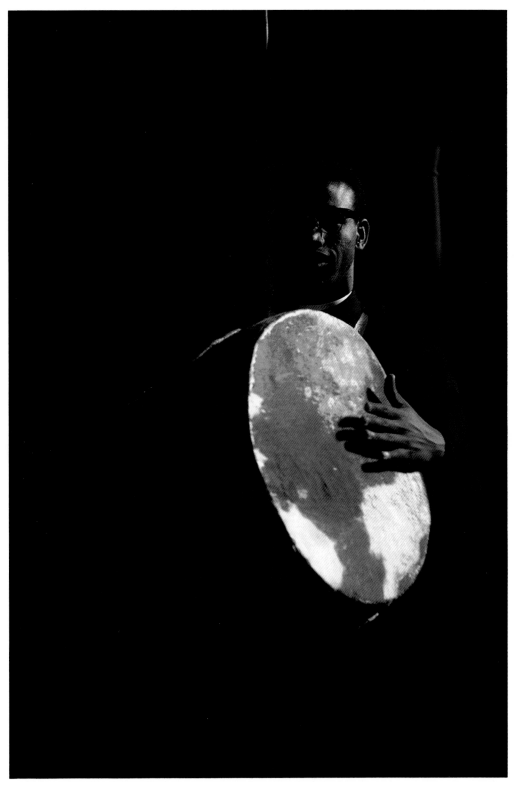

ITALY
An Ethiopian priest drumming for a special
mass at the Vatican

U.S.S.R.
Head of a collective farm in the Kuban

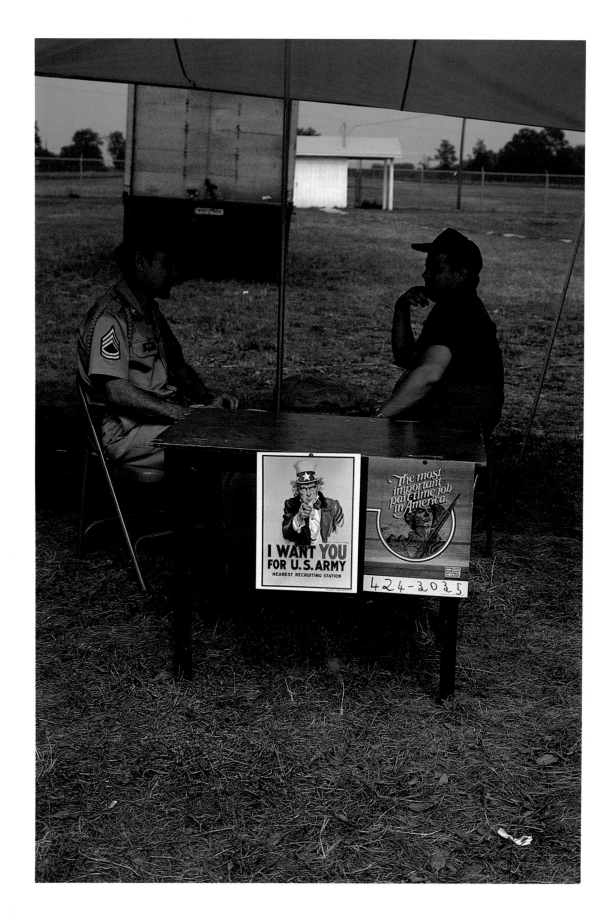

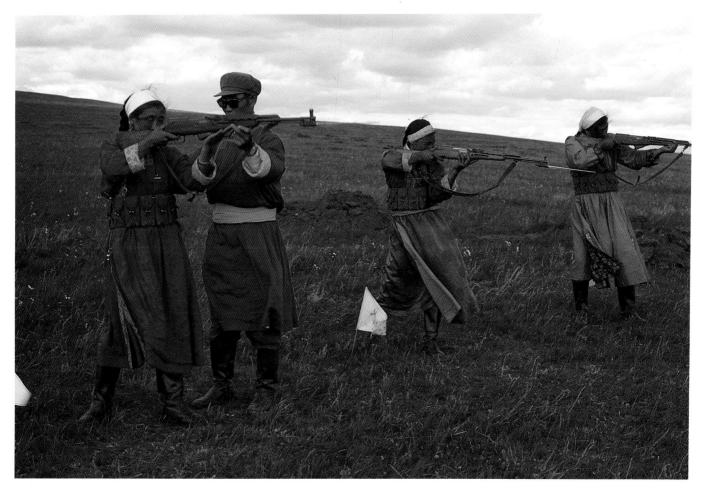

INNER MONGOLIA
Target practice in the grasslands

UNITED STATES
A recruiting team for the U.S. Army

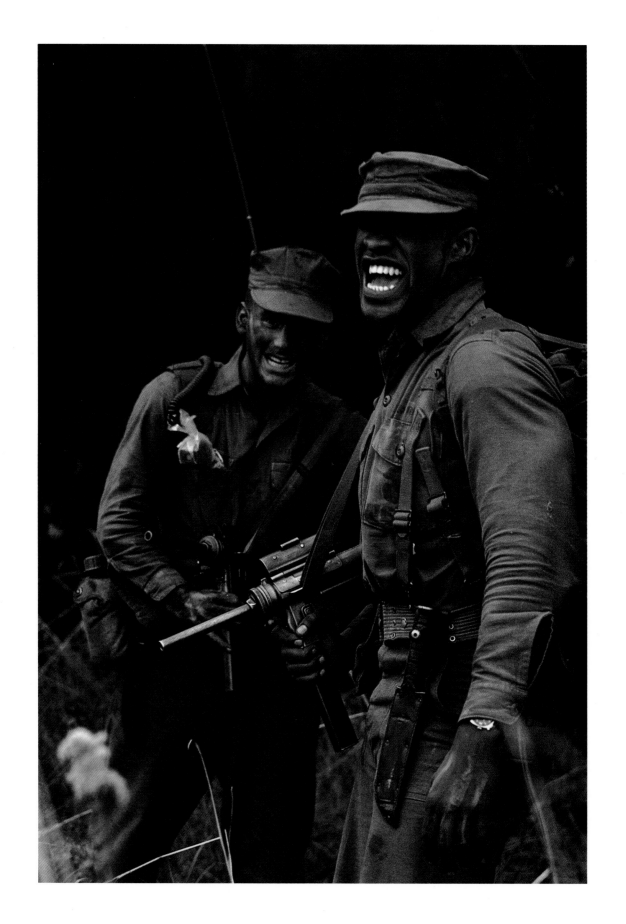

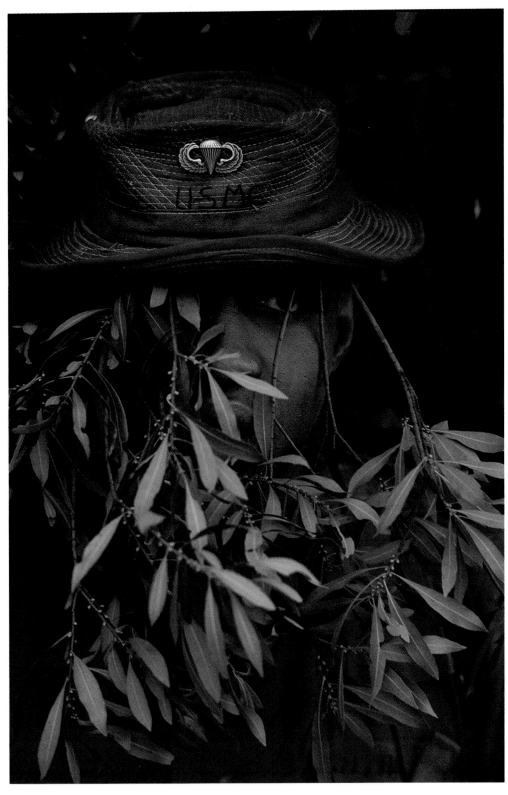

UNITED STATES
A marine teaches camouflage

UNITED STATES
Jungle training for marines

"Whether our work is art or science or the daily work of society, it is only the form in which we explore our experience which is different."

—Jacob Bronowski

England
Studying at the Royal Veterinary College

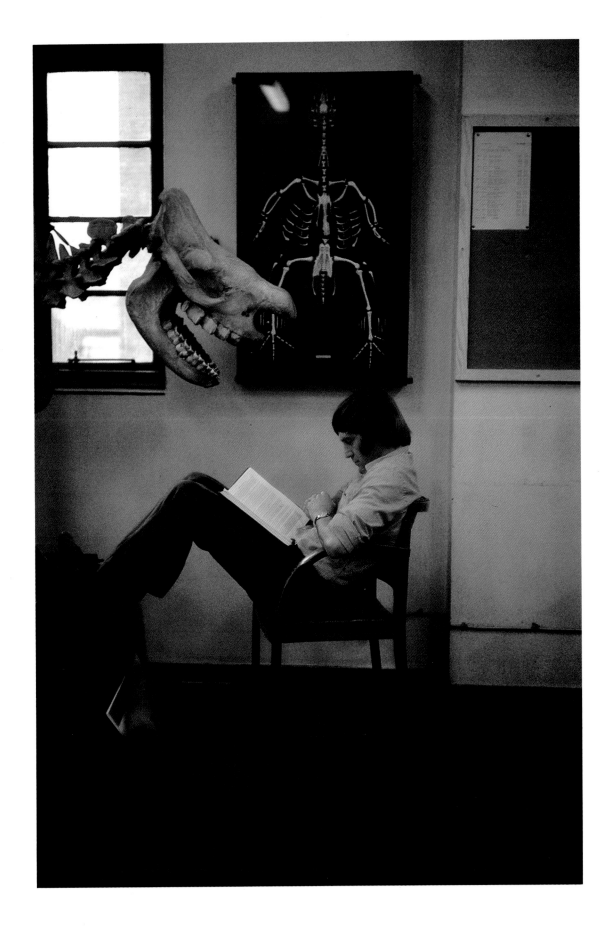

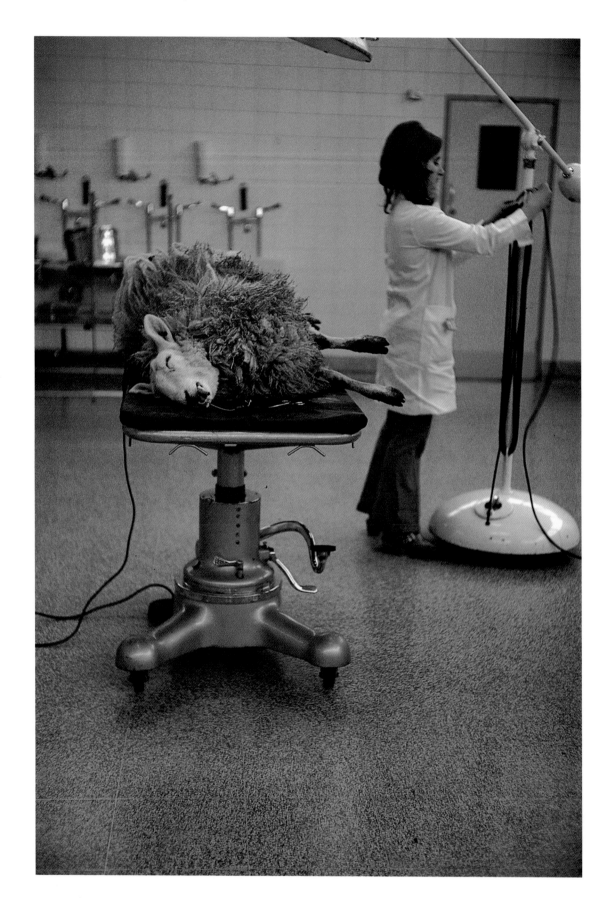

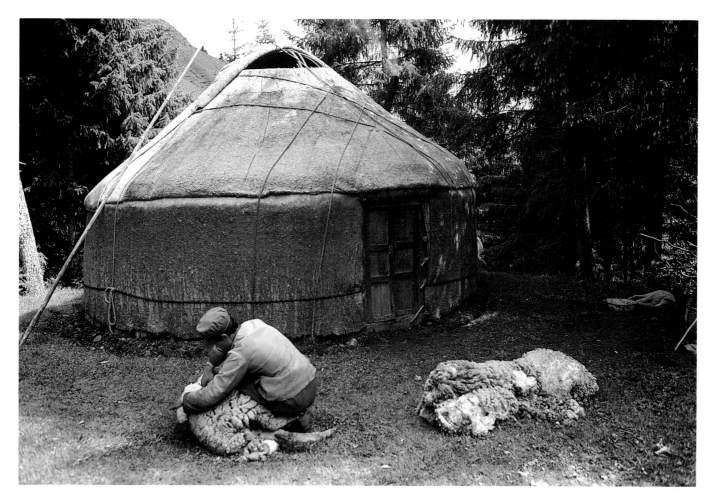

CHINA
Sheepshearing

ENGLAND
At a surgery run by the Royal Veterinary College, a
sheep is prepared for a hysterectomy

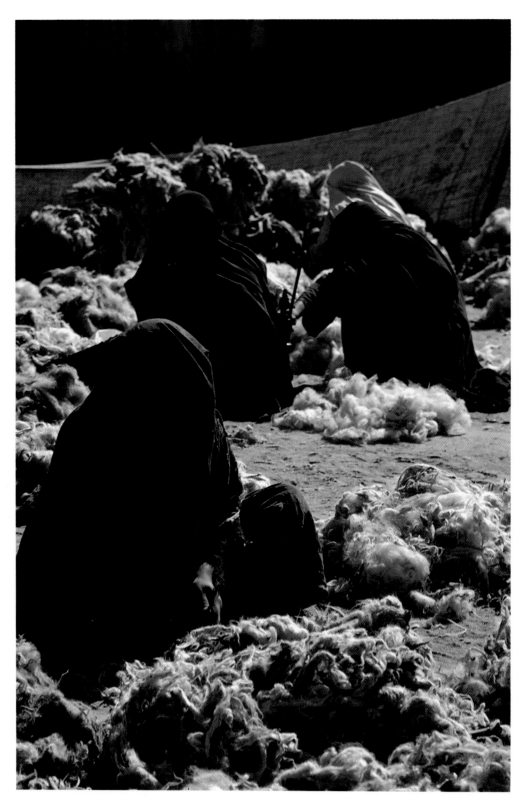

AFGHANISTAN
Women prisoners clean woolen mattress stuffings

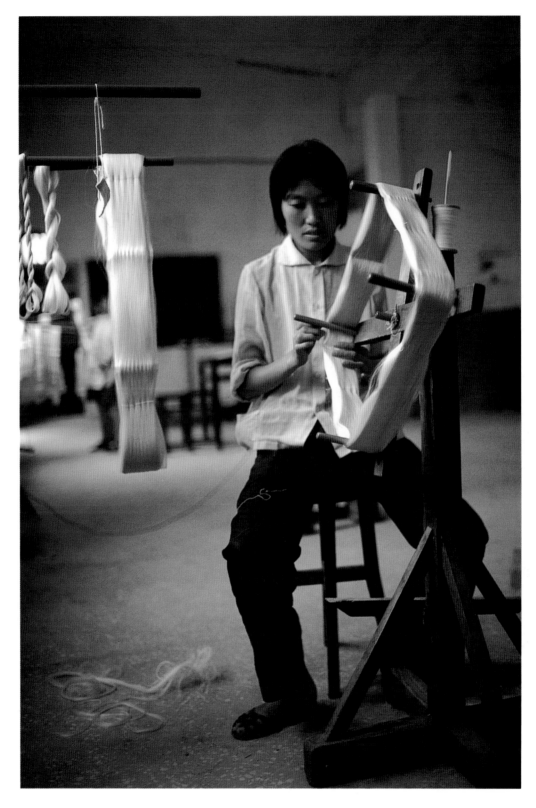

CHINA
Spinning silk

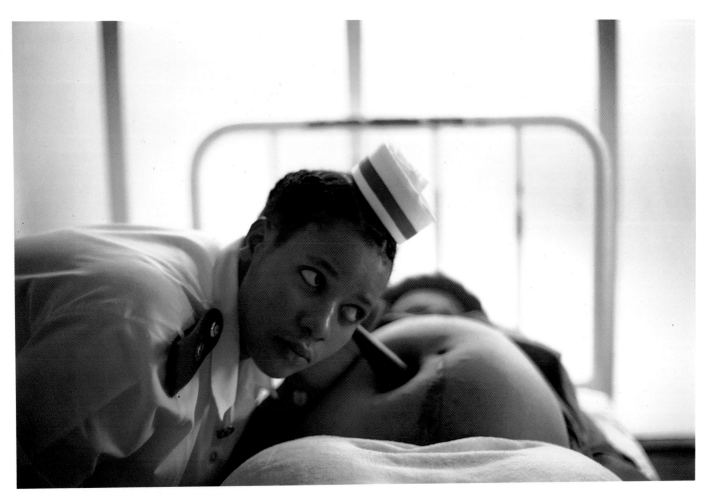

ZULULAND
A nurse listens to a fetal heartbeat

SOUTH AFRICA
Physical examination of a prospective gold miner

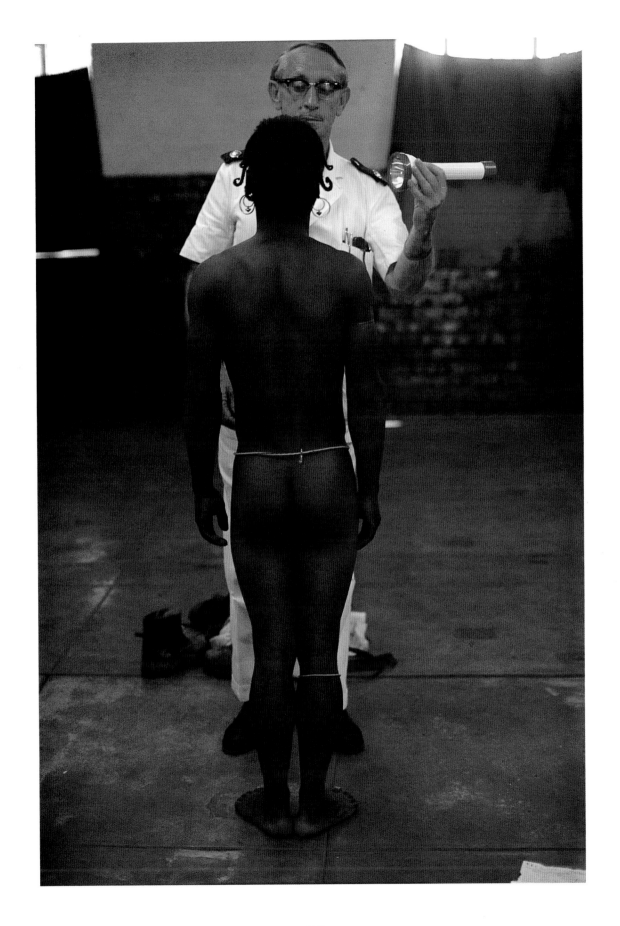

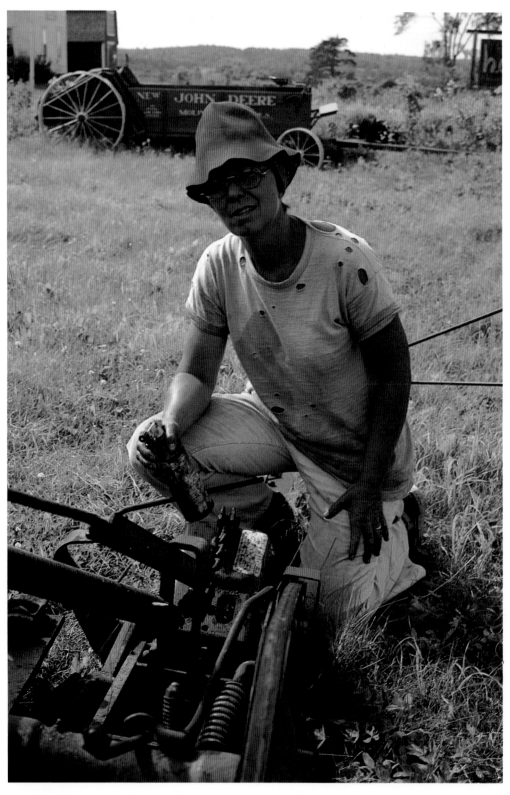

UNITED STATES
A nun doffs her habit to repair the
farm machinery of her order

ENGLAND
A Bride of Christ nun makes her bed

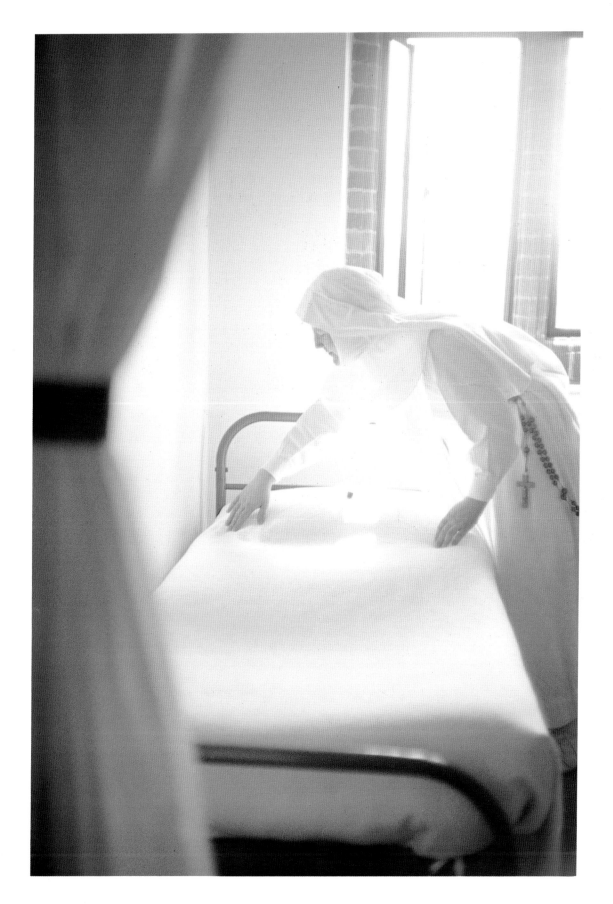

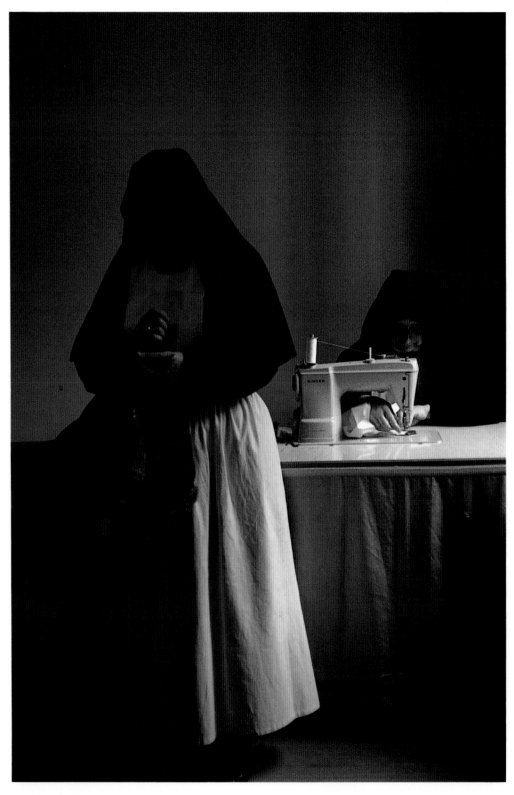

ITALY
Sewing vestments for cardinals
at the Vatican

UNITED STATES
Texas volunteer charity fund-raiser works hard at her donor lists

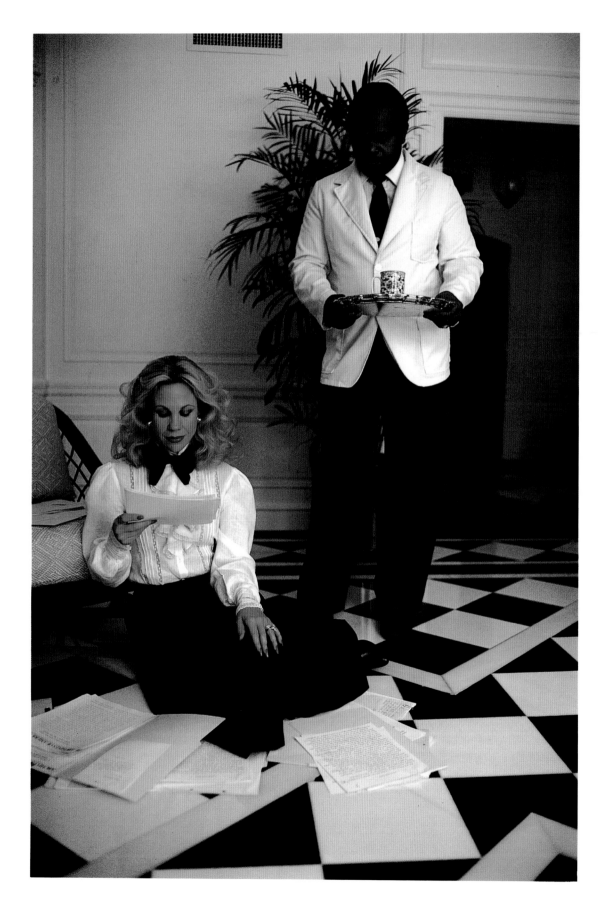

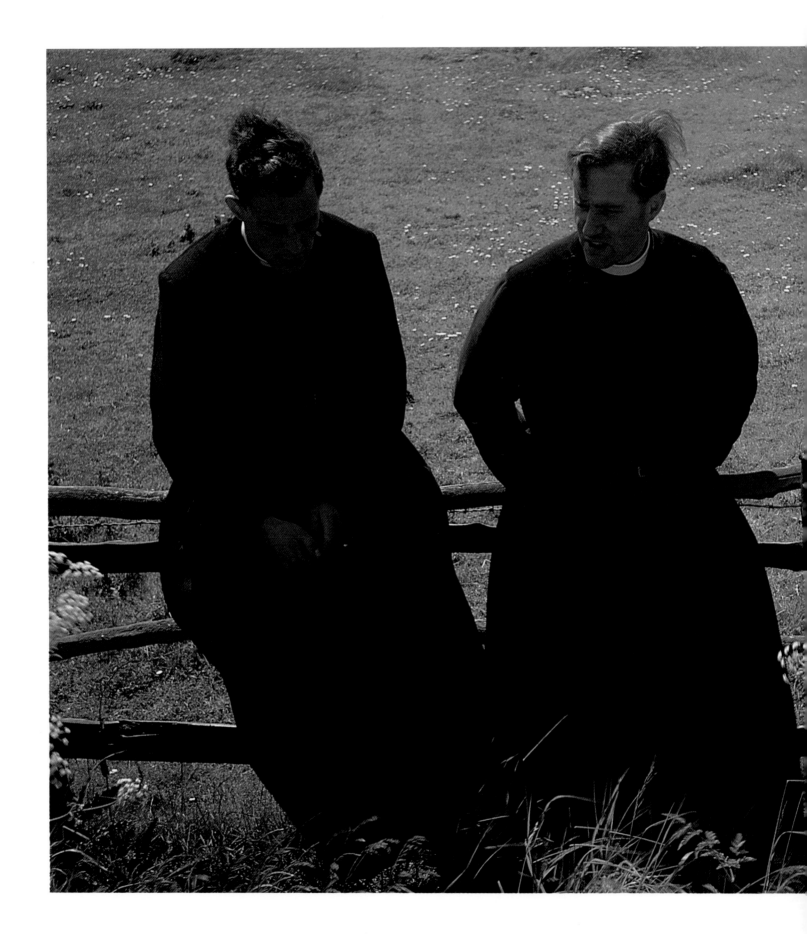

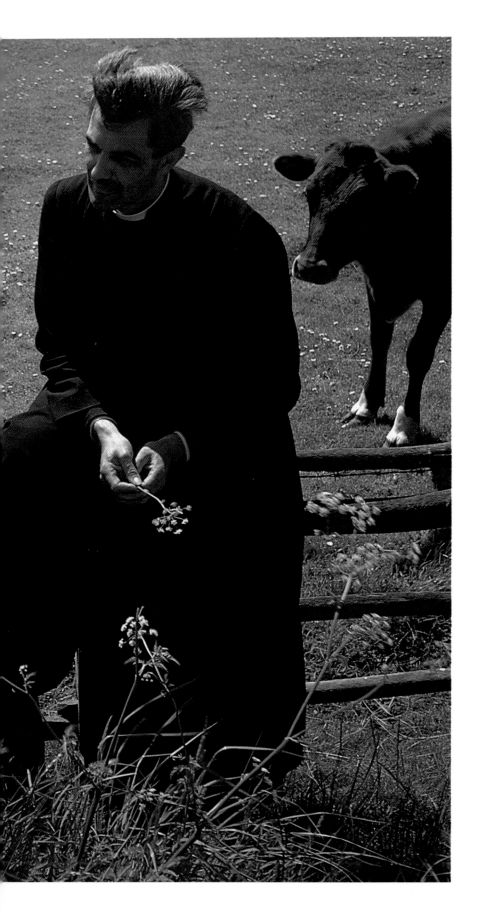

"What is work? and what is not work? are questions that perplex the wisest of men."

—*Bhagavadgita*

ENGLAND
Three vicars from three separate parishes
discuss a common problem

141

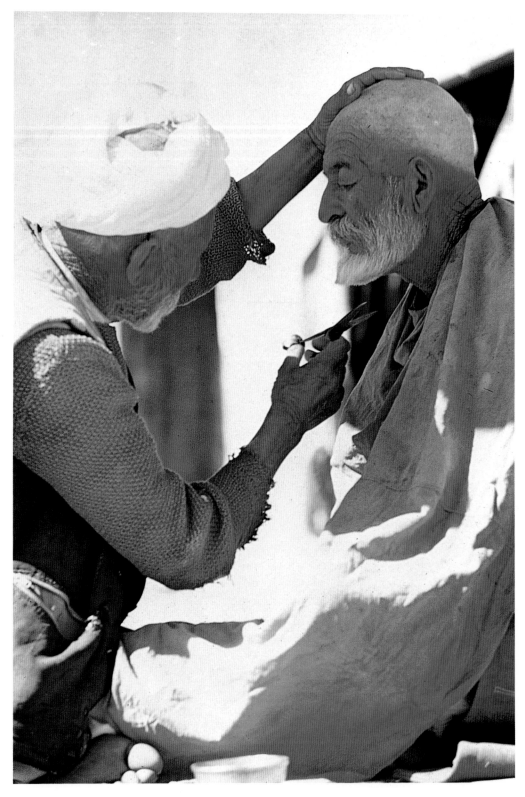

AFGHANISTAN
A barber

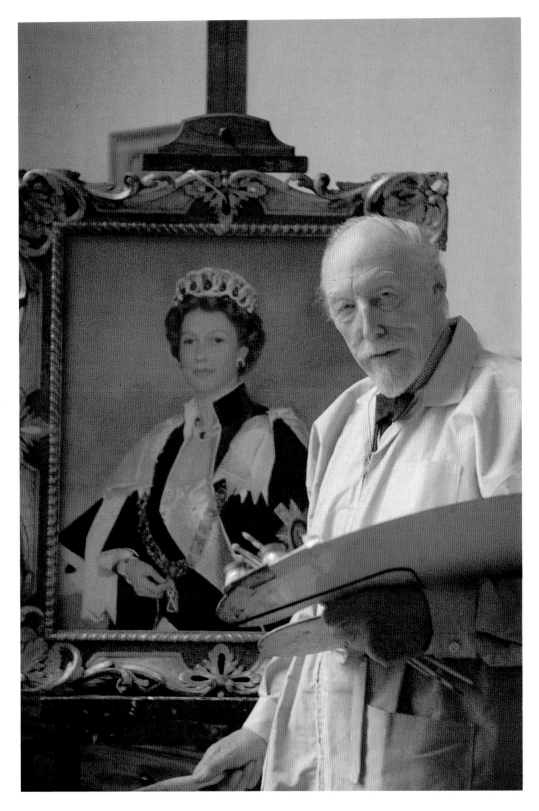

ENGLAND
A member of the Royal Academy displays his portrait of Queen Elizabeth II

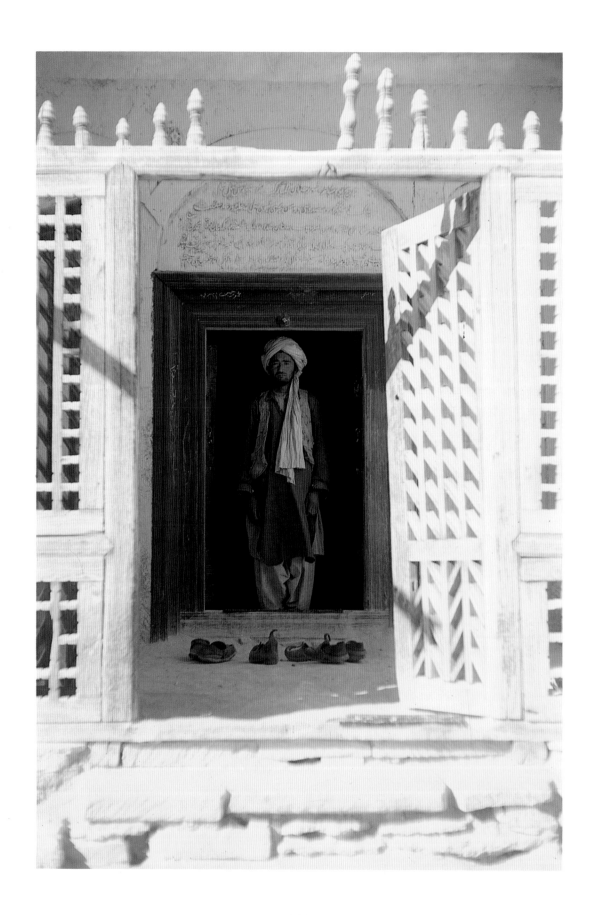

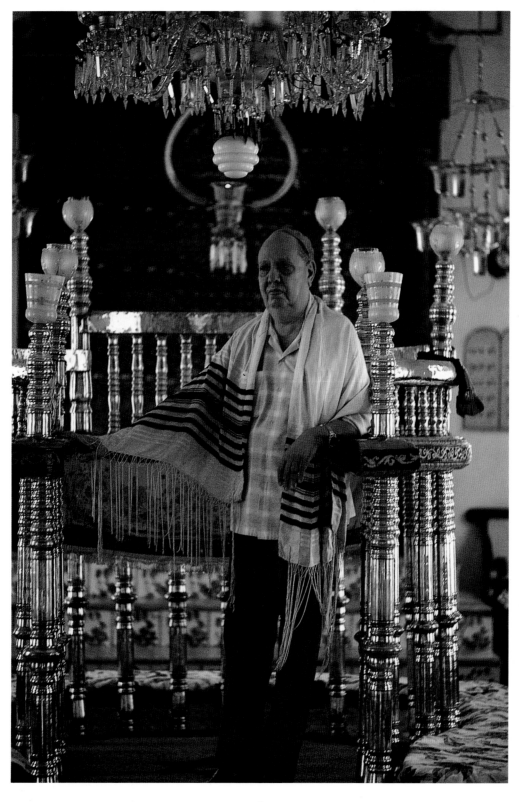

INDIA
A rabbi preaching a sermon at an eighteenth-
century Portuguese synagogue in Cochin

AFGHANISTAN
A beadle in a mosque guards the
footwear of the faithful

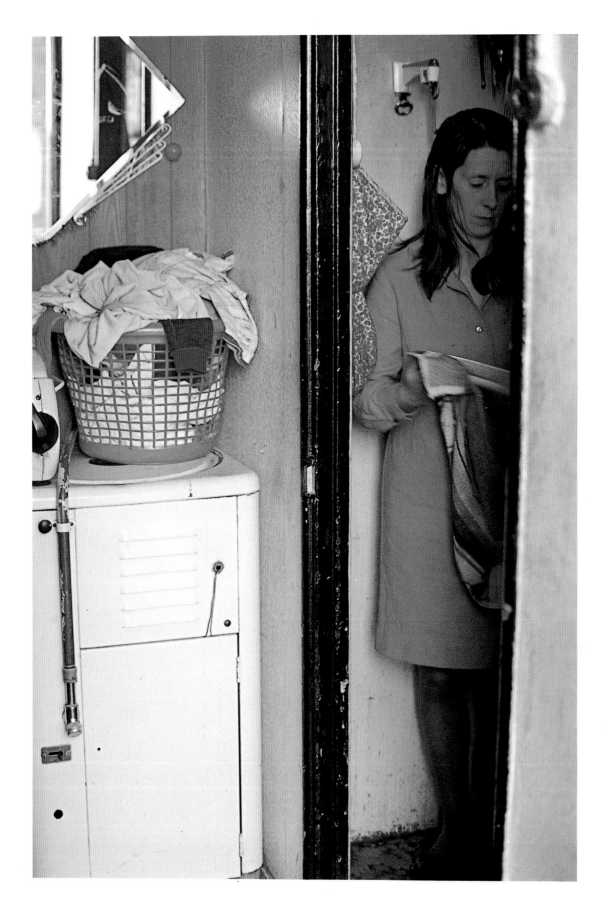

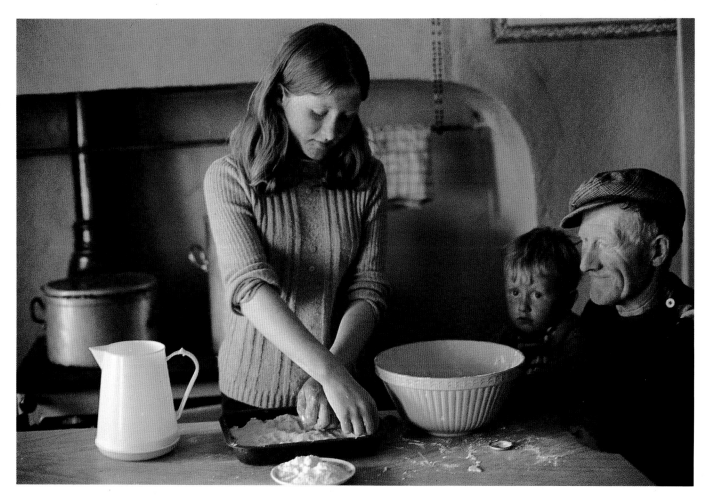

ENGLAND
A British housewife

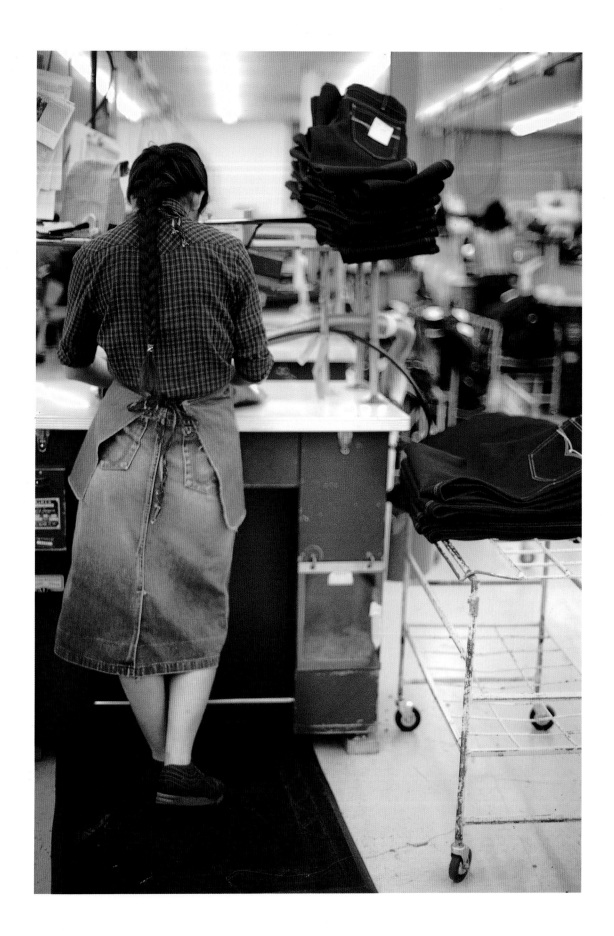

"Work is not the curse, but drudgery is."

—Henry Ward Beecher

149

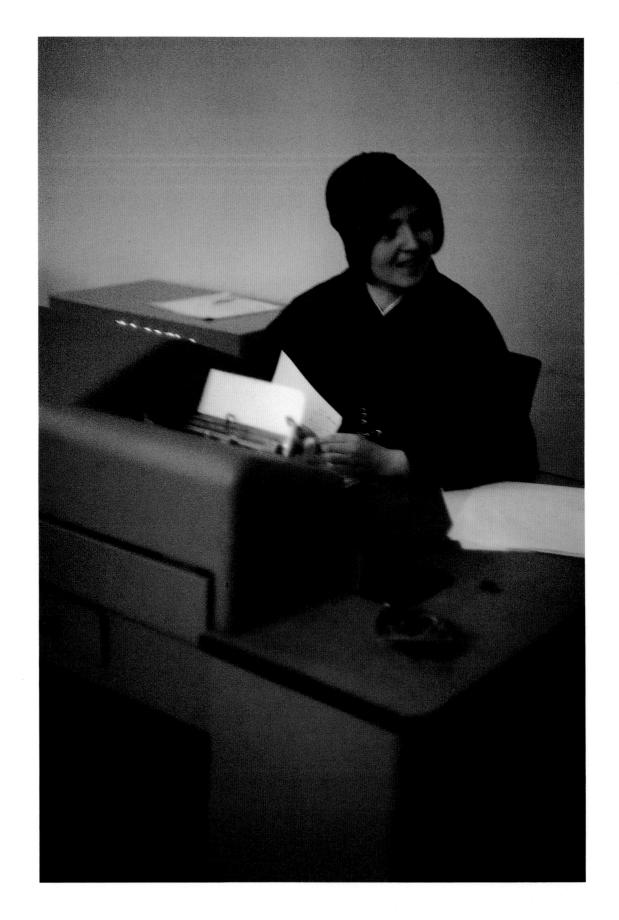

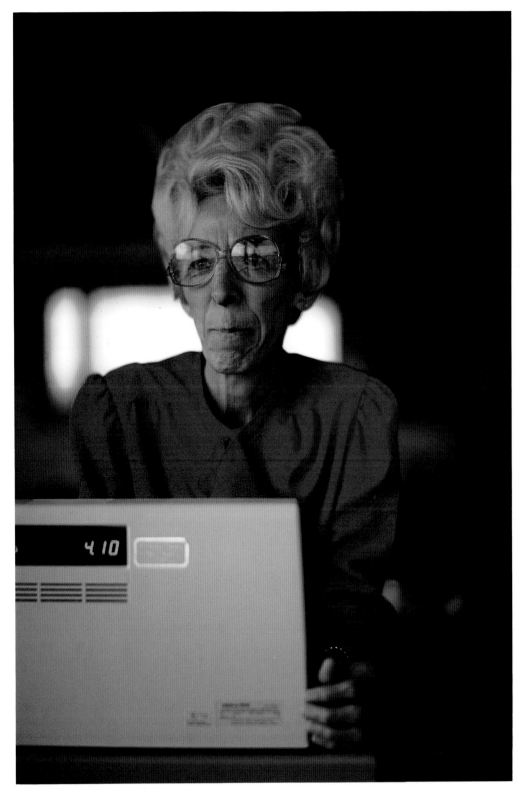

"Most people spend most of their days doing what they do not want to do in order to earn the right, at times, to do what they may desire."

—John Mason Brown

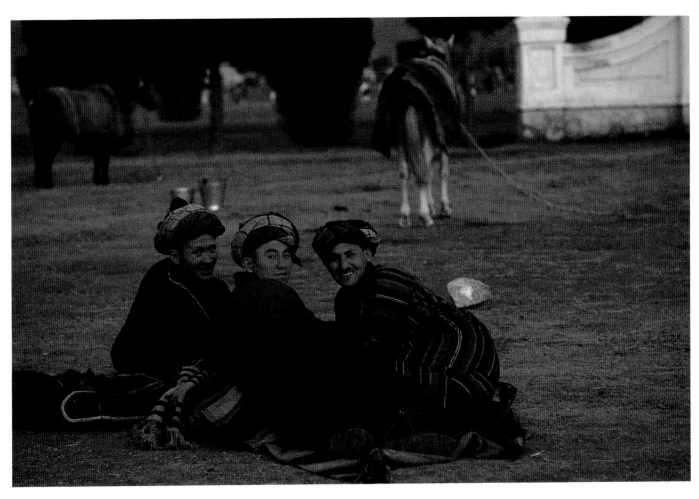

AFGHANISTAN
A trio of professional *buzkashi* riders: the game is
played on horseback with a headless goat or calf

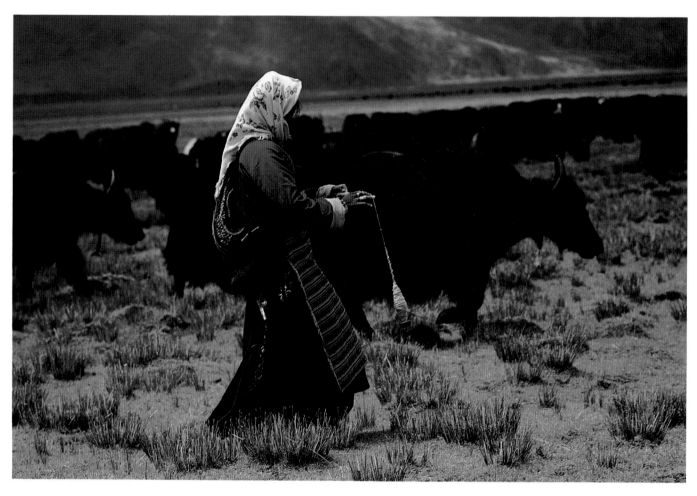

Tibet
Herding yaks

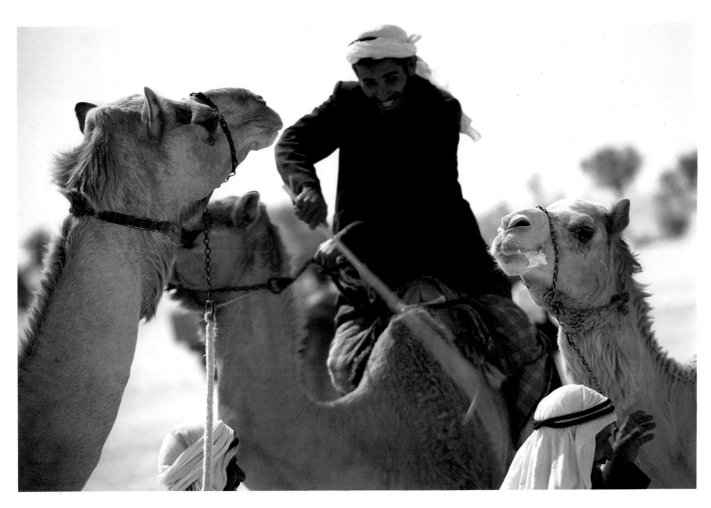

United Arab Emirates
Racing camels in Dubai

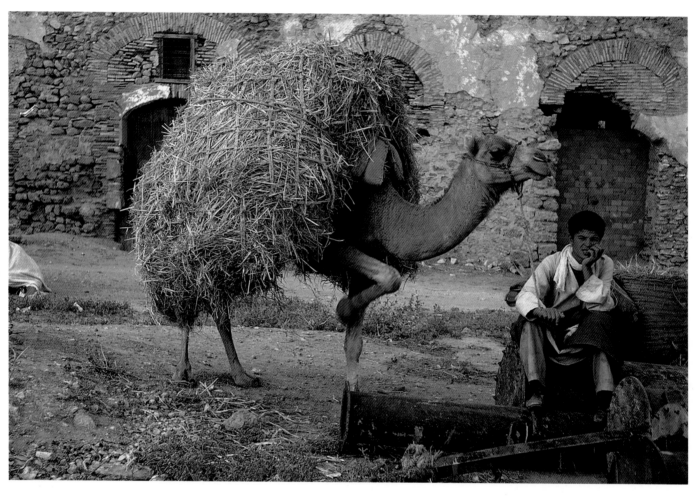

TUNISIA
A camel driver and his animal take a break

U.S.S.R.
One of the oldest men in the world (at age 112)
puts a bridle on a wild horse

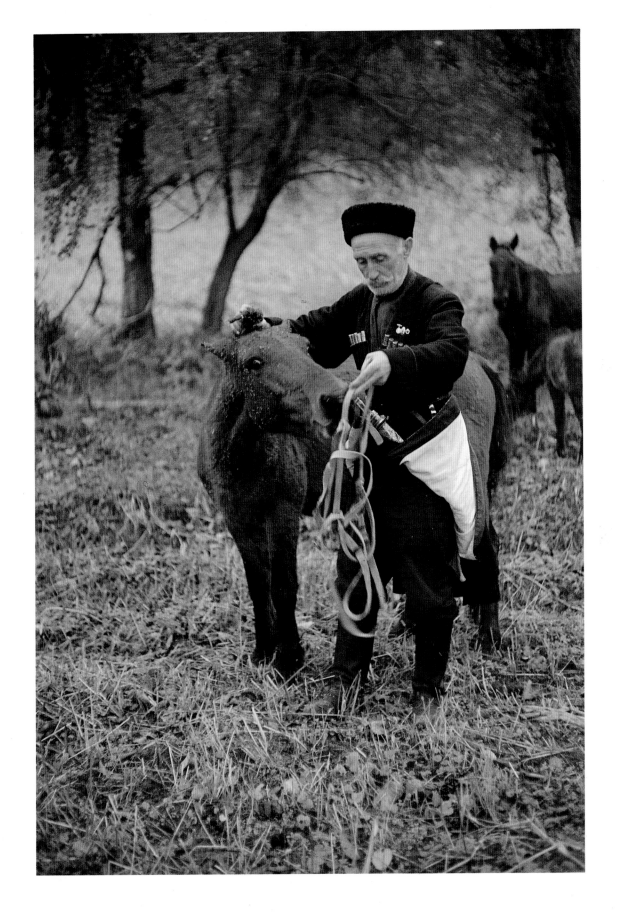

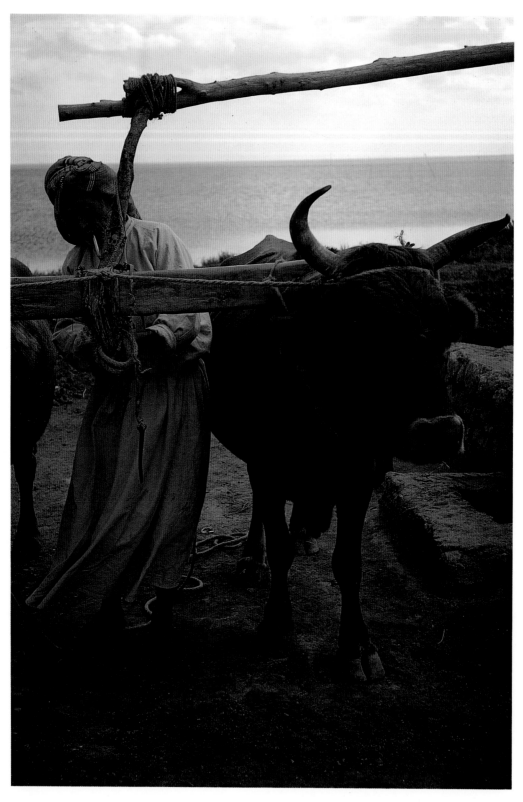

Tunisia
Drawing water from a well

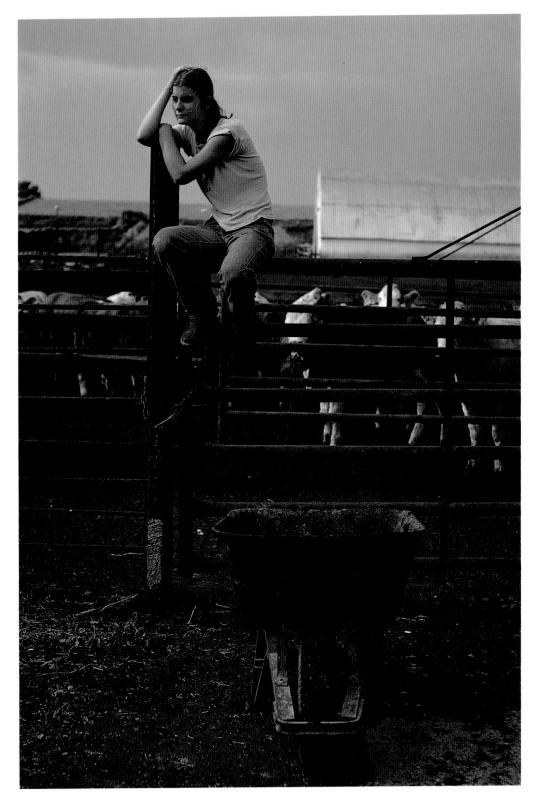

UNITED STATES
A veterinary student with her charges

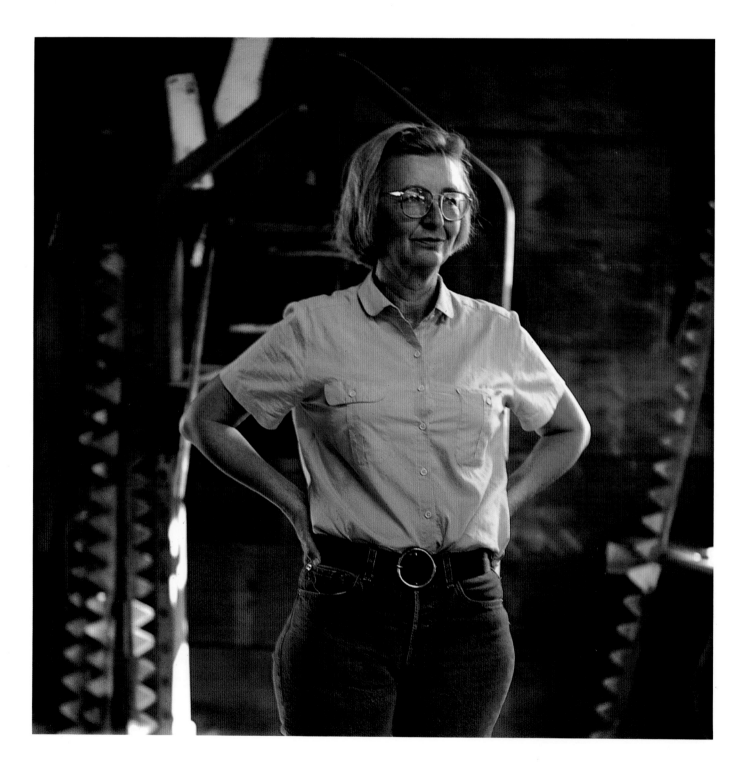

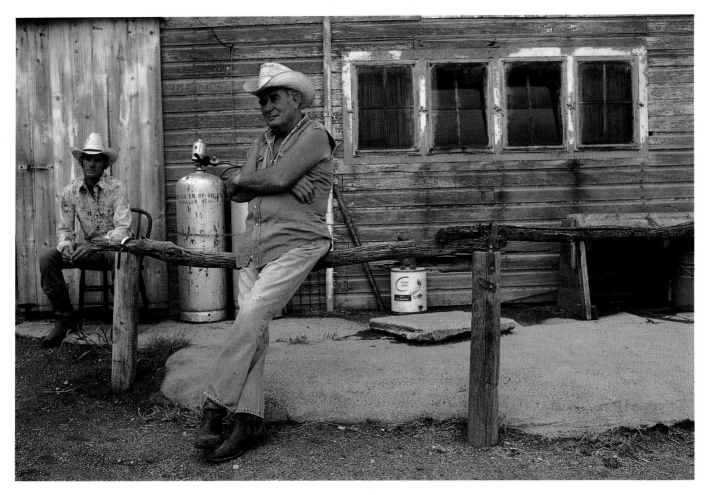

United States
A farmer and his son talk crops

United States
A ranch owner who specializes in artificial
insemination for cattle

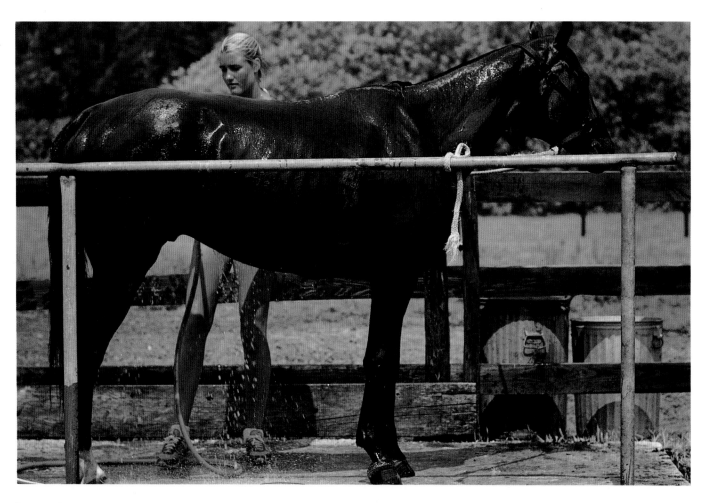

UNITED STATES
Polo player prepares her horse for a match

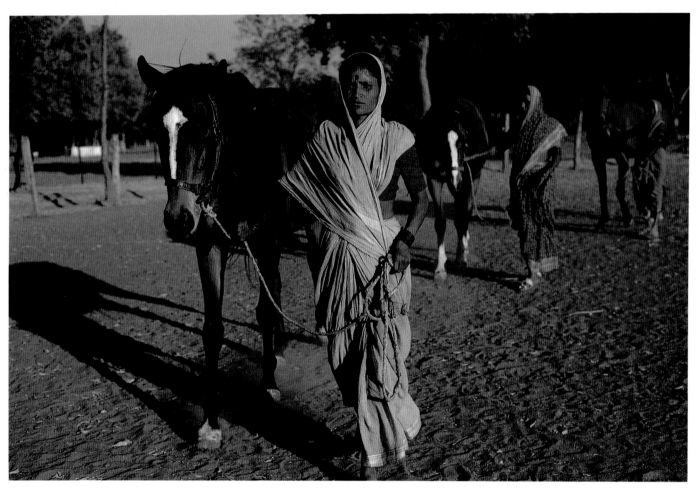

INDIA
Grooms lead their charges toward the stables

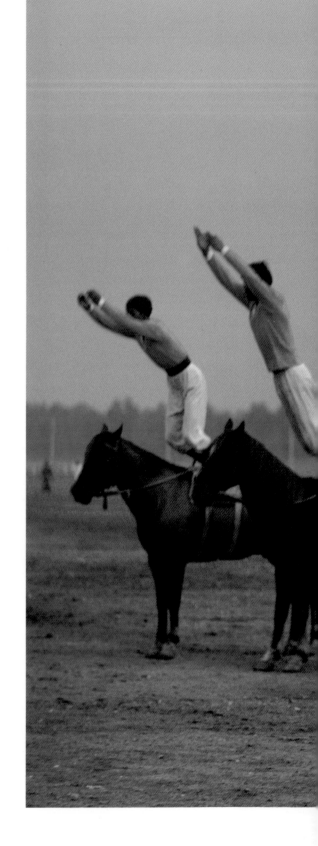

"Do your work with your whole heart and you will succeed—there is so little competition."

—ELBERT HUBBARD

INNER MONGOLIA
Equestrian acrobats rehearsing

164

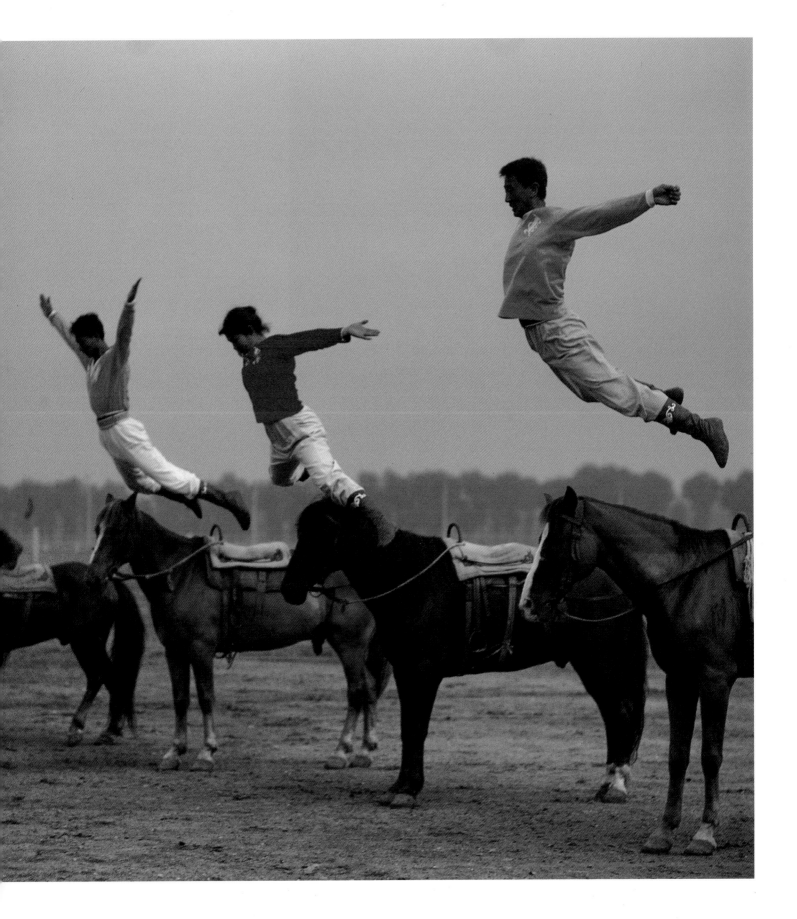

Text and captions set in Schneidler
Display type set in Bauer Text Initials
by TGA Communications, Inc., New York, New York.

The book was printed on 157 gsm Kanzaki Topkote paper
by Toppan Printing Company, Tokyo, Japan.
Bound in Japan by Toppan.